W9-AZG-658

Israel

Frontispiece: Jerusalem is an old city within a modern city.

Consultant: Mitchell G. Bard, PhD, Executive Director, American-Israeli Cooperative Enterprise

Please note: All statistics are as up-to-date as possible at the time of publication.

Book production by Herman Adler Design

Library of Congress Cataloging-in-Publication Data

Hintz, Martin.
Israel, revised edition / by Martin Hintz.— Rev. ed.
p. cm. — (Enchantment of the world. Second series)
Includes bibliographical references and index.
ISBN 0-516-24854-5
1. Israel—Juvenile literature. I. Title. II. Series.
DS126.5.H529 2006
956.94—dc22 2005005705

2 3 4 5 6 7 8 9 10 R 15 14 13 12 11 10 09 08 07

Israel

Revised Edition

BY MARTIN HINTZ

Enchantment of the World
Second Series

Children's Press®
A Division of Scholastic Inc.
NEW YORK TORONTO LONDON AUCKLAND SYDNEY
MEXICO CITY NEW DELHI HONG KONG
DANBURY, CONNECTICUT

Frontispiece: Jerusalem is an old city within a modern city.

Consultant: Mitchell G. Bard, PhD, Executive Director, American-Israeli Cooperative Enterprise

Please note: All statistics are as up-to-date as possible at the time of publication.

Book production by Herman Adler Design

Library of Congress Cataloging-in-Publication Data

Hintz, Martin.
Israel, revised edition / by Martin Hintz.— Rev. ed.
p. cm. — (Enchantment of the world. Second series)
Includes bibliographical references and index.
ISBN 0-516-24854-5
1. Israel—Juvenile literature. I. Title. II. Series.
DS126.5.H529 2006
956.94—dc22 2005005705

3 4 5 6 7 8 9 10 R 15 14 13 12 11 10 09 08 07 62

Acknowledgments

This book is dedicated to the children of Yad Vashem.

For their assistance behind the scenes, as well as their suggestions, tips, and hospitality, the author wishes to thank Geoffrey Weill and his staff at Geoffrey Weill Associates; Israeli Ministry of Tourism officials Aire Sommer, Barbara Sharon Bahny, Martin Davidson, and Tsion Ben David; guide Jeff Abel, who translated his knowledge into easily understandable terms; plus many acquaintances who work in Israeli arts, tourism, science, and politics, including Rachel Grodjinovsky, Katrin Lieberwirth, Asher Weill, Sandy Barkin, Nachman Klieman, Sheryl Stein, and Varda Chassel.

Thanks also to Gil Goldfine, Janet Inbar, Tom Huntington, Ali Halabi, and many other friends who made visits to Israel so productive and valuable, especially Nabeel Naser El-deen, Yona Kalimovitzki, Barbara Liebgott, and Jacob Sudri. And a nod goes to Judean Desert guide Ofer Netzer, who can drive his truck straight up desert cliffsides.

And lastly, thanks to Kathie Bernstein and Jay Hyland of the Milwaukee Jewish Historical Society for their insights.

Cover photo: The Dome of the Rock is visible above the Western Wall of Jerusalem's Second temple.

Contents

Haifa

Elderly Israelis

A Land of Tradition

Beans growing in northern Israel. Irrigation allows crops to be grown throughout much of this dry country.

The Negev Desert in southern Israel is a parched land of multicolored rock, wind-shifted sand, and scrub brush. A caravan of four-wheel-drive vans inches across the harsh landscape, kicking up a dust cloud. The vehicles seem to move across a vast lake, but the shimmering waters are only a mirage. The trucks are packed with eager tourists interested in learning about Israel's wilderness. Cameras ready, they are alert for any subject that might make a photo to brag about at home.

Deep underneath the rugged hills, a valuable reservoir of natural springs supports the hardy vegetation sprouting amid the boulders. In the distance, irrigated fields are dazzlingly green. Towering date palms guard against the encroaching sand.

Opposite: **These burial structures in the Negev Desert are six thousand years old.**

The Dome of the Rock was completed in 691. This Muslim shrine is in the middle of the Temple Mount, the holiest site in Judaism.

Old and New

Although the visitors are far out in the desert, they are never really too distant from Israel's modern cities and extended suburbs. Israel is a tiny country, snuggled along the Mediterranean Sea and surrounded on three sides by Egypt, Jordan, Syria, and Lebanon. Its towns and villages are a mix of the ancient and modern, where trendy nightclubs sit next to famous historical sites. Grizzled old vendors peer out from their market stalls down the street from upscale shopping malls.

Israel is a sacred land for many faiths. The vast Dome of the Rock, which overlooks Jerusalem, is the site where Muhammad, the founder of Islam, is said to have ascended into Paradise. The Second Temple was the center of Jewish worship when it was built in Jerusalem 2,500 years ago. It was destroyed in A.D. 70. At the Western Wall, the remnants of the Second Temple's retaining wall, Jews today run their fingers along the sun-drenched stones as they pray. Nearby are the holiest shrines of Christianity. Christian pilgrims come from around the world to be baptized in the Jordan River. Their white robes billow as the muddy water surges around them.

On the Mediterranean coast, modern Tel Aviv bustles with traffic and people. Its sidewalk cafés; glittering office buildings; art museums; world-famous opera and theater; and wide, tree-lined avenues showcase it as a city on the move. Schoolchildren dash through the streets, talking and shouting with their friends.

Around the cities and settlements, Israelis are turning the dry desert into a fertile countryside. Jets of water spray from irrigation hoses, gracefully arcing over plump, ripe melons waiting to be picked. The ragged fronds of date palms dance in

Israelis relaxing at an outdoor café in Tel Aviv. Israel is full of lively cities.

a midday breeze. Not far away, fishers cast their nets across the calm waters of the Sea of Galilee. The only visible difference between the scene today and a similar one a thousand years ago is the outboard motor powering each tiny boat.

Near Solomon's Pools, south of Jerusalem, shepherd boys scramble their long-eared donkeys up and over the low ridges. Ahead of them are flocks of black and white sheep grazing on the dry grass. Far to the north, near the Lebanese border, other kids play ice hockey at the Canada Centre, a Canadian-built sports center in Metulla.

The three reservoirs known as Solomon's Pools are near Bethlehem, in the West Bank. They were built more than two thousand years ago.

Palestinians burn an Israeli flag during a protest at a refugee camp in Syria. Nearly four hundred thousand Palestinian refugees live in Syria.

A Young Nation

Although Israel has an ancient history, it is a young nation. It only became an independent state in 1948. In the decades before and after, millions of Jews, many facing violence and hatred elsewhere, emigrated to the area that is now Israel. They considered it both a safe haven and their spiritual homeland.

The region is also home to millions of Palestinians, most of whom are Muslim (followers of Islam). In the turmoil following the creation of Israel, many Palestinians fled their homes. Some ended up in nearby Arab countries such as Jordan and Lebanon. Others live in the West Bank and the Gaza Strip,

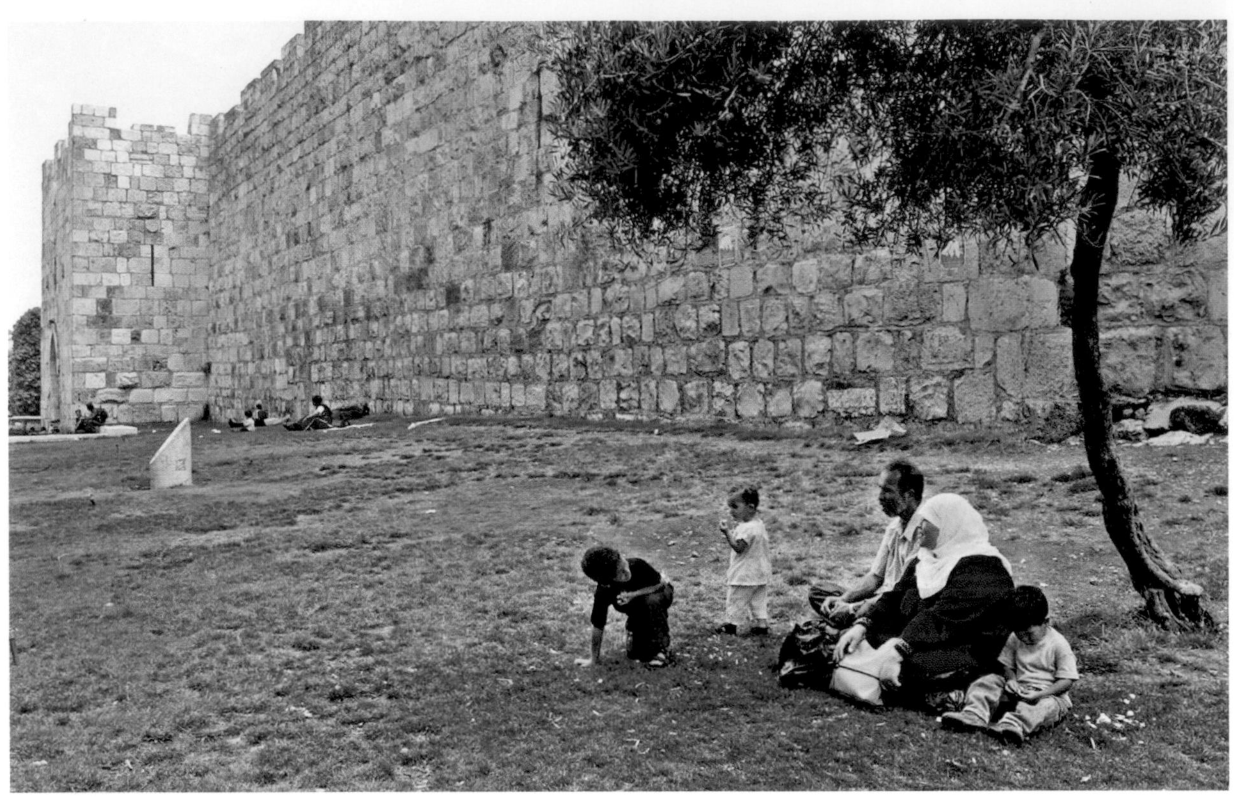

An Arab family sits near the wall that surrounds Jerusalem's Old City. Jerusalem is a holy city for Muslims, Jews, and Christians.

areas next to Israel that have been central to the violent, long-running conflict between Israelis and Palestinians. The region is a startling mix of contrasts: it is filled with ancient holy sites, so important to so many, and it is the frequent site of horrific violence. The thought of Israel often brings to mind bombed-out buses, stone-throwing crowds, and gun-toting soldiers.

To its citizens, Israel is more than merely a country. It is a state of mind, an emotion, and a melting pot of differing dreams and opposing aspirations. Despite the turmoil, the hardy young nation remains a place of enthusiasm, optimism, concern, and faith.

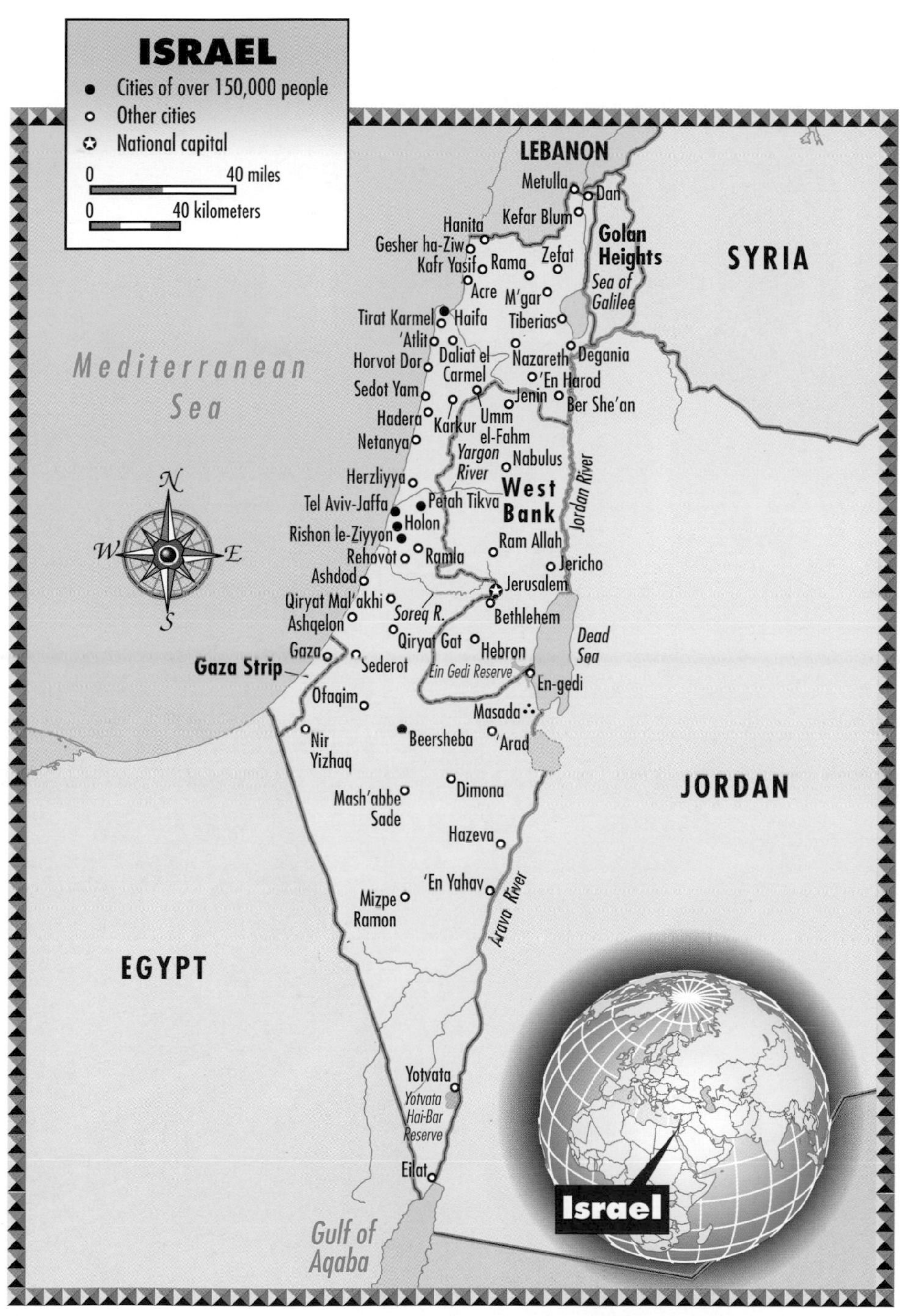
ISRAEL
Cities of over 150,000 people
Other cities
National capital
0
40 miles
0
40 kilometers
LEBANON
SYRIA
JORDAN
EGYPT
Mediterranean Sea
Gulf of Aqaba
Golan Heights
West Bank
Gaza Strip
Sea of Galilee
Dead Sea
Jordan River
Yargon River
Soreq R.
Arava River
Ein Gedi Reserve
Yotvata Hai-Bar Reserve
Metulla
Dan
Kefar Blum
Hanita
Gesher ha-Ziw
Kafr Yasif
Rama
Zefat
Acre
M'gar
Tirat Karmel
Haifa
Tiberias
'Atlit
Horvot Dor
Daliat el Carmel
Nazareth
Degania
'En Harod
Sedot Yam
Jenin
Ber She'an
Hadera
Karkur
Umm el-Fahm
Netanya
Nabulus
Herzliyya
Tel Aviv-Jaffa
Petah Tikva
Holon
Rishon le-Ziyyon
Rehovot
Ramla
Ram Allah
Jericho
Ashdod
Jerusalem
Qiryat Mal'akhi
Ashqelon
Bethlehem
Qiryat Gat
Hebron
Gaza
Sederot
En-gedi
Ofaqim
Masada
Nir Yizhaq
Beersheba
'Arad
Dimona
Mash'abbe Sade
Hazeva
'En Yahav
Mizpe Ramon
Yotvata
Eilat
N
S
E
W
Israel

TWO

Blooms in the Desert

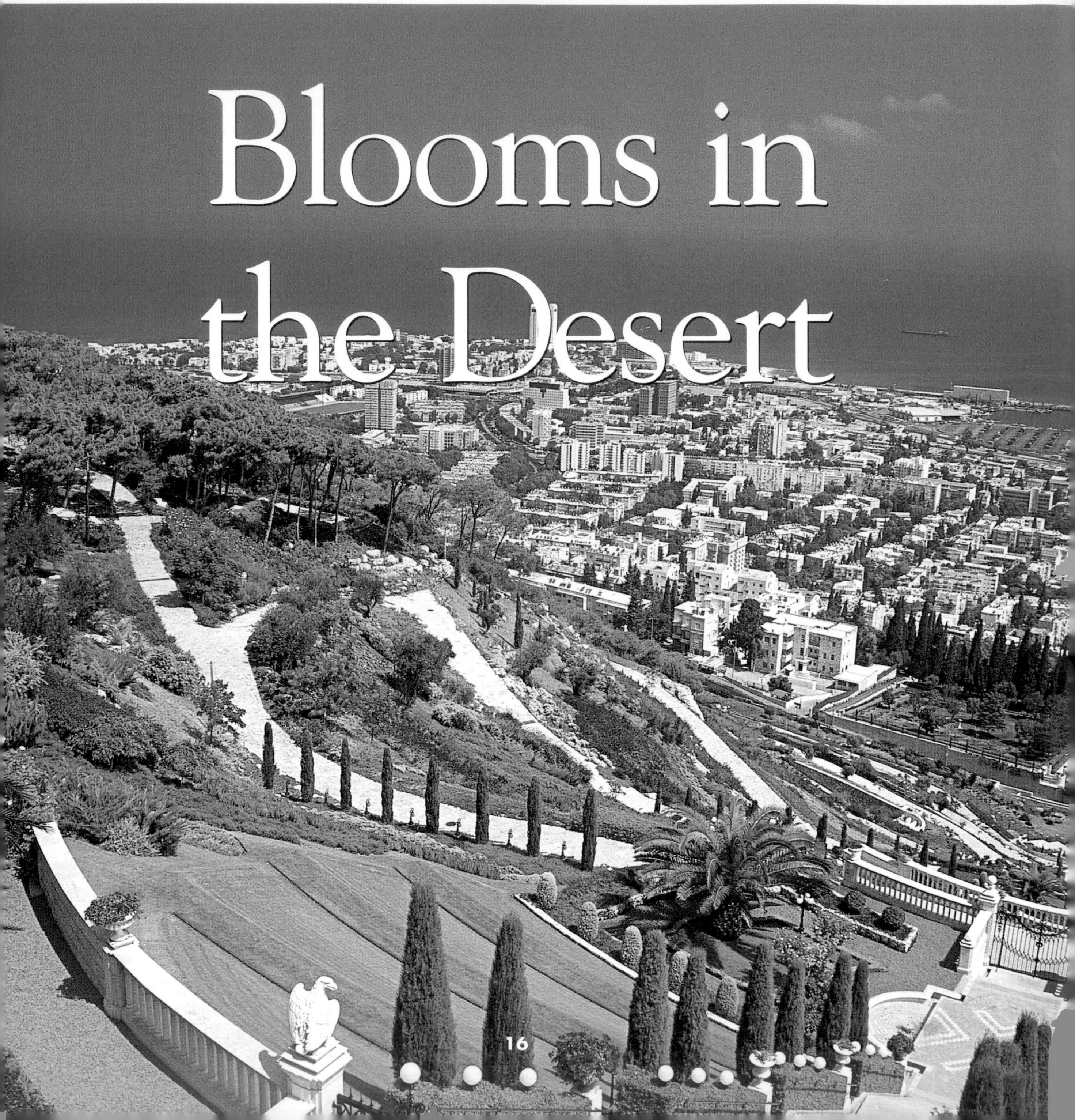

Israel is a wedge-shaped country that borders the Mediterranean Sea. Egypt lies to the southwest, Lebanon to the north, Jordan to the east, and Syria to the northeast. Israel is only a bit larger than the state of New Jersey. It is 290 miles (470 kilometers) long and about 85 miles (135 km) across its widest point.

Opposite: **A view of Haifa from the Baha'i shrine**

Israel's Borders

The amount of territory controlled by Israel changes as the political situation in the region changes and as negotiations continue between the Israelis and their Arab neighbors. In 2004, the country's area totaled 7,849 square miles (20,330 sq km). This included the Golan Heights—an area that has traditionally been part of Syria but which Israel now controls—and East Jerusalem, which Palestinians consider part of the West Bank.

Israel has a scenic coastline that meanders along cliffs and sandy beaches for 170 miles (274 km). It has a 165-mile (266 km) border with Egypt; a 32-mile (51 km) border along the Gaza

The Golan Heights is to the northwest of Israel. The area was captured by Israel in 1967 during the Six-Day War.

Strip; a 148-mile (238 km) border with Jordan; a 49-mile (79 km) border with Lebanon; a 47-mile (76 km) border with Syria in the Golan Heights area; and a 191-mile (307 km) border on the West Bank.

Since a war in 1967, Israel has controlled the Gaza Strip, which borders Egypt and the Mediterranean Sea, and the West Bank, which borders Jordan. Under recent agreements negotiated with the Palestinians, Israel gave up control over much of these lands to the Palestinian Authority, a political body that administers areas controlled by the Palestinians. Israel has withdrawn from all of Gaza, but Jewish settlements in the West Bank are still expanding.

Boats at the harbor in Gaza. In recent years, the Palestinian Authority has gained some self-government in the Gaza Strip.

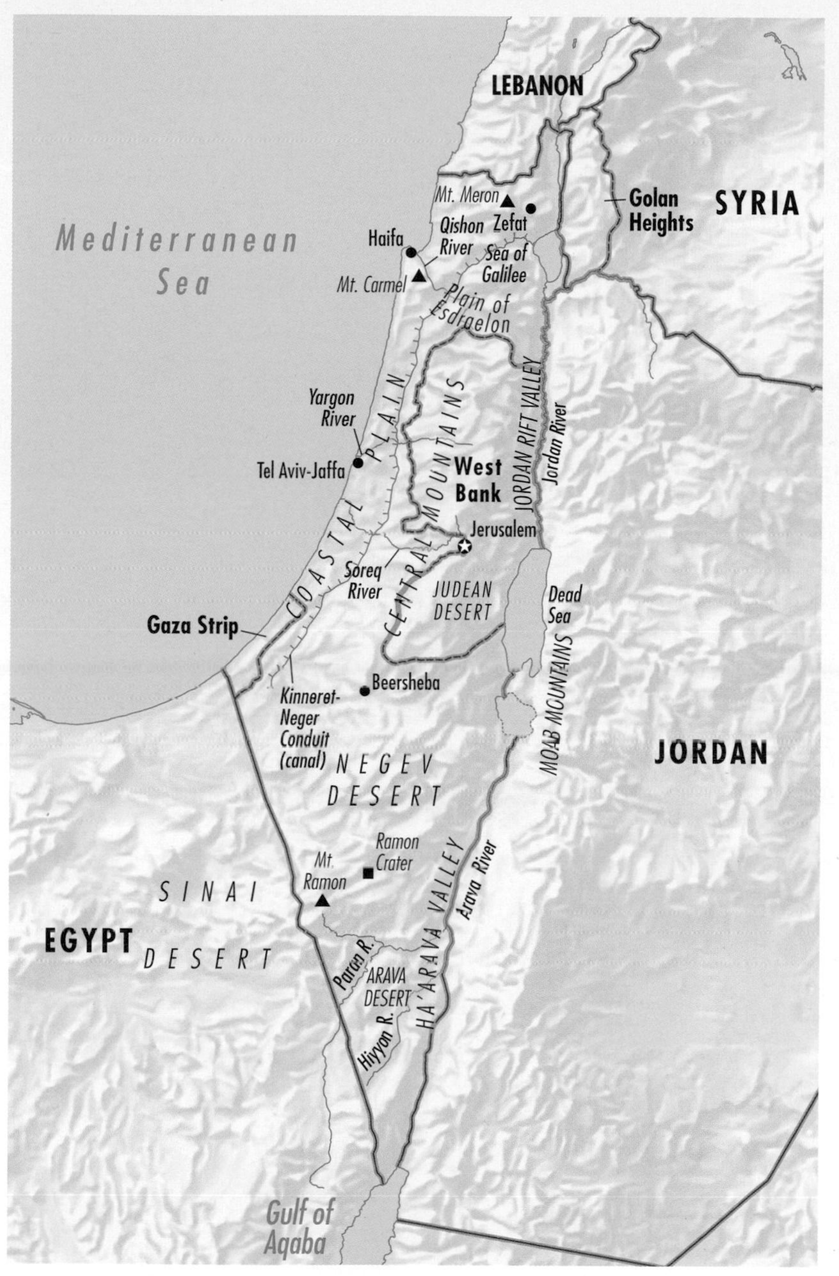

Israel's Geographical Features

Highest Elevation: Mount Meron, 3,963 feet (1,208 m)

Lowest Elevation: Dead Sea, 1,312 feet (400 m) below sea level

Longest River: Jordan River, 186 miles (299 km)

Widest Lake: Sea of Galilee, 64 square miles (166 square km)

Largest City: Jerusalem, population 680,500 (2004, includes East Jerusalem)

Highest Recorded Temperature: 129°F (54°C)

Area: 7,849 square miles (20,327 sq km)

Average Annual Rainfall: 28 inches (71 cm) in the north and 2 inches (5 cm) in the south

The Arbel Valley lies west of the Sea of Galilee in northern Israel. Many people enjoy hiking or biking through the Arbel countryside.

Where Israelis Live

Israel is made up of four distinct sections. The coastal plain in the west includes the cities of Haifa and Tel Aviv. It is home to much of Israel's agriculture and industry. The Valley Region to the east includes the Jordan River, which links the Sea of Galilee and the Dead Sea. A third area of Israel lies in the north and includes the Galilee, Samaria, and Judea. This highland region includes Israel's highest point, Mount Meron, at 3,963 feet (1,208 meters) tall. The highlands are also home to Jerusalem, which lies on rocky land in the Judean Hills. Most Israelis live in these three sections. The southern deserts are the fourth section.

Deserts in the South

The southern part of Israel consists of the sprawling Negev and Arava red-sand deserts. The Negev Desert is bordered by a coastal plain that lies along the Mediterranean Sea to the north, the Sinai Desert to the west in Egypt, the Moab Mountains to the east, and the Judean Desert to the northeast. The Negev was traditionally too arid for farming, but in parts of the desert, irrigation systems have been set up that allow crops to thrive. The Ramon Crater, in the center of the Negev, is one of the world's largest natural craters at 5 miles (8 km) wide, 25 miles (40 km) long, and about 1,600 feet (500 m) deep. It was formed over millions of years as water wore away the earth. The Arava Desert is southeast of the Negev and stretches along Israel's border with Jordan.

The Arava Desert spreads out across southeastern Israel. This dry region supports little plant life.

Looking at Israel's Cities

Tel Aviv (below), the second-largest city in Israel, is the nation's business center. In 2004, the population of Tel Aviv and the ancient city of Jaffa that borders it was 360,500. Tel Aviv's cultural attractions include the Golda Meir Center for the Performing Arts and the Tel Aviv Museum of Art. The promenade along the beach is a favorite place for joggers and strollers. Tel Aviv is known as the "city that never stops" because of its nightclubs, coffeehouses, and discos. The city was founded in 1909 as one of the first Jewish urban centers in the area. Temperatures in January range from 48 to 63 degrees Fahrenheit (9 to 17 degrees Celsius) and in August are from 72° to 85°F (22° to 29°C).

The old part of the city of Haifa was founded four thousand years ago. Today, 270,800 people live in Haifa, a leading cultural and entertainment center. It is home to the Haifa Municipal Theater, the Tikutin Art Museum, and a large soccer stadium. Haifa's population is diverse, and the city is known for its tradition of sheltering religious minorities. In fact, it is the largest Israeli city to have a mixed population of Jews and Arabs. A Baha'i temple—the world headquarters of this faith—stands on a hillside overlooking downtown.

Beersheba began as a camel market for Bedouins, desert-dwelling Arabs who traditionally moved from place to place. Today, it is a vacation site and one of Israel's largest cities, with a population of 181,500. The Ben-Gurion University of the Negev in Beersheba, founded in 1969, was named after Israel's first prime minister. The Israel Air Force Museum and the weekly Bedouin market are other attractions. The city is the jumping-off point for exploring the Negev Desert.

Zefat (above), at 3,200 feet (975 m) above sea level, is the city "closest to heaven"—the highest in Israel. Zefat is the birthplace of the kabbalah—the teachings of Jewish mysticism—and is one of the four holy cities of Judaism. The first book in Hebrew was printed here in 1578. Dozens of artists have studios and galleries in this city of 27,000. The temperature ranges from 31 to 48°F (–1 to 9°C) in January and from 66 to 84°F (19 to 29°C) in August.

The Dead Sea is the saltiest and most mineral-rich body of water on Earth. Many visitors come to the Dead Sea for its health and beauty benefits.

Salty Water

The Dead Sea is actually a lake, and it is not really dead. At least eleven types of bacteria are found in its waters. But no other forms of life can survive in these waters, which are about nine times as salty as the ocean. Many people enjoy floating in the Dead Sea because the dense salt-filled water holds them up easily.

The Dead Sea is shrinking at the rate of several feet a year. This is partly because of evaporation and partly because water from the Jordan River, which feeds into the Dead Sea, is being diverted for irrigation. The lake provides many natural resources. Bromine, magnesium chloride, and potash are taken from the lake and used for health care products and in other industries.

The clear, blue-green lake is 34 miles (55 km) long and ranges from 2 to 11 miles (3 to 18 km) wide. Its waters are as much as 1,373 feet (418 m) deep. At 1,312 feet (400 m) below sea level, the Dead Sea is lower than any other lake on Earth. Ears pop as motorists descend the long stretch of highway to the Dead Sea from Jerusalem, which is 2,400 feet (732 m) above sea level.

A 110-passenger ship, *Lot's Wife*, putt-putts across the dense waters of the Dead Sea. The vessel is made of wood because metal cannot withstand the sea's high salt and mineral content. The ship is named for the woman who, in the Bible, disobeyed an angel's order not to look back on the destruction of the cities of Sodom and Gomorrah. She was turned into a pillar of salt for her curiosity and disobedience.

Famous Waterways

Although the Jordan River is only 186 miles (299 km) long, it is one of the most famous waterways in the world. It was often mentioned in the Bible and is notable for its religious significance. The Jordan originates in the mountains of southern Lebanon and Syria and flows south through Israel to the Dead Sea, sometimes forming part of the border with Jordan. It also feeds and drains the Sea of Galilee.

The river's steep-sided valley, called the Jordan Rift Valley, is 2 to 15 miles (3 to 24 km) wide. Most of the river's course is below sea level. During the hot summers, when the temperature hits 100°F (38°C), the water narrows to a stream. Many Israelis enjoy white-water rafting in the few stretches of wild, rock-cluttered water. Dams on the lower Jordan provide electric power.

The Sea of Galilee is historically and religiously important. It is a small lake, only about 13 miles (21 km) long and 7 miles (11 km) wide, with a depth of 155 feet (47 m). Fish thrive in its cold waters. While the sea is usually calm, downdrafts of cold air off the nearby hills can cause violent storms. A Bible story tells of Jesus walking on its raging surface, thereby quieting the storm. The area surrounding the Sea of Galilee is quite beautiful. In the rainy winter, the countryside is filled with cypress and colorful wildflowers. Ruins of ancient Greek and Roman cities encircle the lake, and the region has been a popular getaway spot for centuries.

The city of Tiberias lies along the Sea of Galilee. It is one of Israel's most popular vacation spots.

CHAPTER THREE

The Natural World

Israel is one of the few nations in the world where it is against the law to pick wildflowers. Picking flowers was once a popular pastime in Israel, but some plants almost became extinct because they were so popular. Many groups work hard to ensure that future generations of Israelis will be able to enjoy the country's forests, mountains, waterfalls, and beaches. Even the deserts are important. The Negev Center for Regional Development was established in 1993 to study and control the impact of the many people moving into the great southern desert. The Ministry of Environment is responsible for monitoring Israel's air, water, and land to make certain the activities of a modern society do not damage the natural world.

Opposite: **Wildflowers carpet an Israeli hillside.**

The Nubian ibex lives in the northern Negev Desert. Its horns can grow 4 feet (1.2 m) long.

Safe Places

Even as Israel spreads out from its cities, a few remote areas remain where wild creatures can live in relative peace. The mountain gazelle leaps from ridge to ridge in the high hills. Nubian ibex race across the plains. Agama lizards and chameleons scurry among the desert rocks. To protect threatened plant and animal species, the Israelis have established the Nature

Reserves Authority, which oversees 150 havens for animals and plants. One such site is the Hula Nature Reserve in Upper Galilee near the city of Zefat. There are also three *hai-bar* reserves in the country. *Hai-bar* means "wild life" in Hebrew, the national language of Israel.

The Hai-Bar National Biblical Wildlife Reserve, the largest of the three, lies on 8,000 acres (3,200 hectares) near the Jordanian border. The Negev Desert creeps around the edges of this oasis, which is home to creatures mentioned in the Scriptures. The reserve also holds a breeding center that tries to raise enough animals so that some can be released into the wild.

The Hula Valley is home to a nature reserve where tens of thousands of birds, including storks, pelicans, and herons, make their home.

Somali wild asses are about 4 feet (1.2 m) tall at the shoulder. They are the smallest wild equid, the group of animals that includes horses, zebras, and asses.

One such animal is the white oryx, a large, fleet-footed African antelope with long straight horns that project backward. Popular with hunters for centuries, the white oryx was hunted almost to extinction until Hai-Bar began raising them in its safe environment. On the reserve's wide savanna, or plain, Somali wild asses also run free. With their striped legs, they look as if they could be a zebra's cousin. Brought to Hai-Bar from Iran, the asses had been extinct in Israel for two thousand years.

Some animals arrived at Hai-Bar in unusual ways. Mesopotamian fallow deer were smuggled in from Iran in the 1970s during a violent revolution in that country. Rare ostrich chicks were flown out of war- and drought-ravaged Ethiopia by the Israeli Air Force.

The red, big-eared fennec fox also roams the Hai-Bar reserve. This furry little fellow is the tiniest member of the fox family. The swift, lanky southern wolf also calls the reserve its home. Scientists have put collars with electronic devices on the wolves so they can be tracked with radio equipment. Tracing the wolves' movement broadens knowledge of how these elusive animals live.

The fennec fox digs burrows in the sand where it remains during the day. It hunts for its prey of small mammals, insects, lizards, and birds at night.

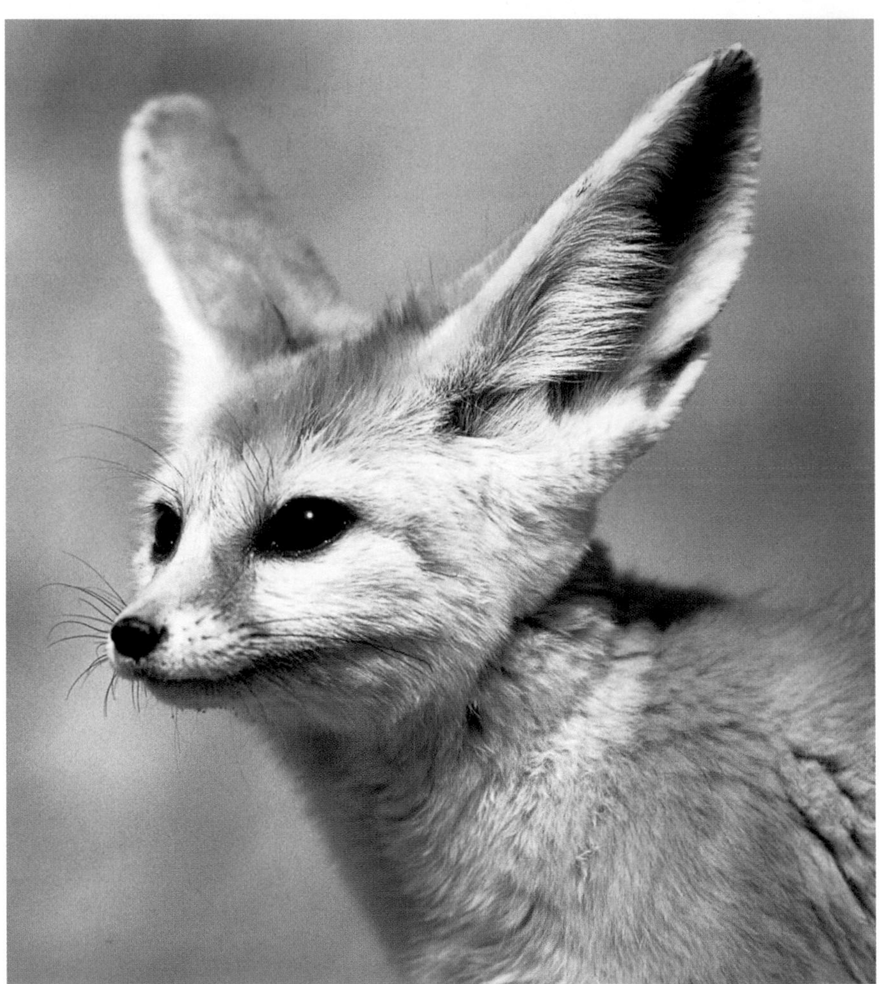

Birdlife

Birds flock everywhere in Israel. The common bulbul, Sylvia warbler, goldcrest, and a variety of hawks and falcons are full-time residents. The International Birdwatching Center near Eilat enables scientists who study birds to observe the hundreds of thousands of birds that live in the region. Area birdwatchers are kept busy. They identify honey buzzards and many other birds that migrate to and from Africa in March and October.

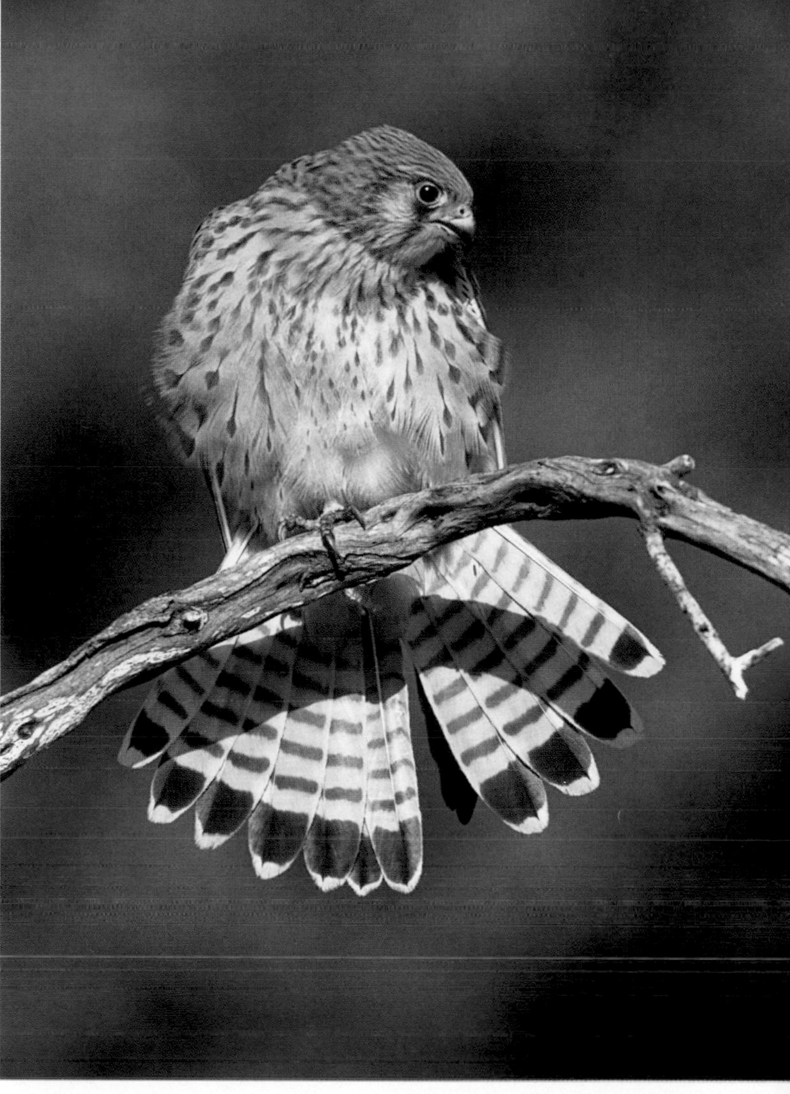

The lesser kestrel is a small falcon. Each summer, about five hundred pairs of lesser kestrels settle in Israel to breed.

Working Animals

Donkeys, horses, and camels are used regularly in Israel. Every Thursday, Bedouins gather at the bustling sheep, goat, and camel market at Beersheba, the largest city in the Negev Desert. Buyers and sellers haggle over prices. The open square is dusty and loud from the cries of the various animals.

Arab, Bedouin, and Druze shepherds train the sharp-eyed Canaan dog to round up their flocks. This tough breed, which dates back thousands of years, can trot for hours over the harsh landscape.

Prize of the Desert

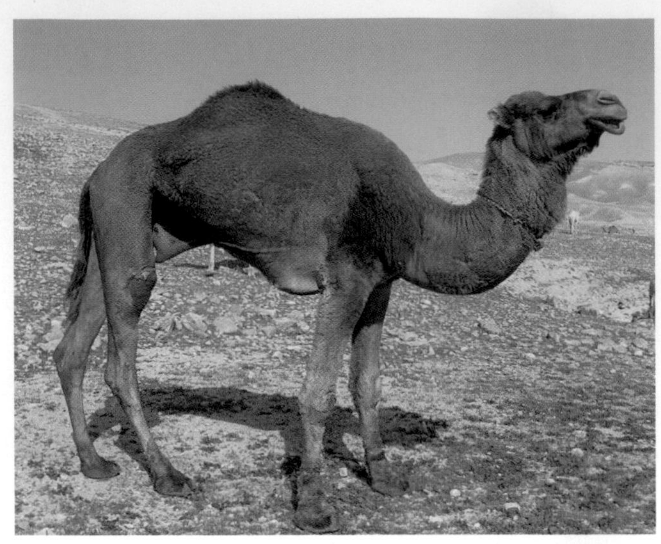

The camel remains the most prized animal in the desert. Camels have been domesticated for thousands of years. They are used for carrying heavy loads and for transporting people across desert land. Their meat is good to eat, and their milk is delicious. In fact, camel's milk is the only kind of milk that does not curdle.

A camel can store up to 1.5 gallons (5.7 liters) of water in the cells of its body, enough to last it for about three days. The camel's face is perfect for protecting the animal in the harsh desert. Its long eyelashes keep out the blowing sand, and its eyelids and nose funnel rainwater to its mouth. Fat is stored in the humps on its back. The dromedary, or one-humped camel, is the most common in the Middle East. It has short hair; long, skinny legs; and wide pads on its sensitive feet that enable it to cross sandy terrain. Camels are usually 6 to 7 feet (1.8 to 2.1 m) tall at the shoulder. They can trot for many hours at about 9 miles (14.5 km) per hour.

Planting Trees

In 1901, before Israel became an independent nation, the Jewish National Fund was founded to purchase land in the region. It also tried to reclaim forests. By the time Israel became independent in 1948, the fund had purchased 240,000 acres (97,000 hectares) and planted 4.5 million trees on the boulder-strewn hillsides. By the early 2000s, more than 220 million trees had been planted, covering 300,000 acres (120,000 hectares). Many of the trees are oak, which were a major part of the biblical landscape. Carob, terbinth, cypress, eucalyptus, Judas, acacia, olive, pine, and almond trees have also been planted.

Each winter, Israelis celebrate *Tu B'shvat*. This is the "new year of trees," a holiday of tree planting. Israelis of all ages turn out for planting ceremonies.

Most cities have extensive gardens in parks and along roads. The country's hot sun brings out the rich colors of flowers and bushes. To view native plants from various parts of the country, Israelis enjoy visiting the extensive gardens of Neot Kedumim, a biblical landscape reserve in the center of Israel.

The Neot Kedumim Biblical Landscape Reserve attempts to recreate the landscapes mentioned in the Bible. The reserve also has guides who demonstrate how people lived in biblical times.

CHAPTER

FOUR

From the Past to Tomorrow

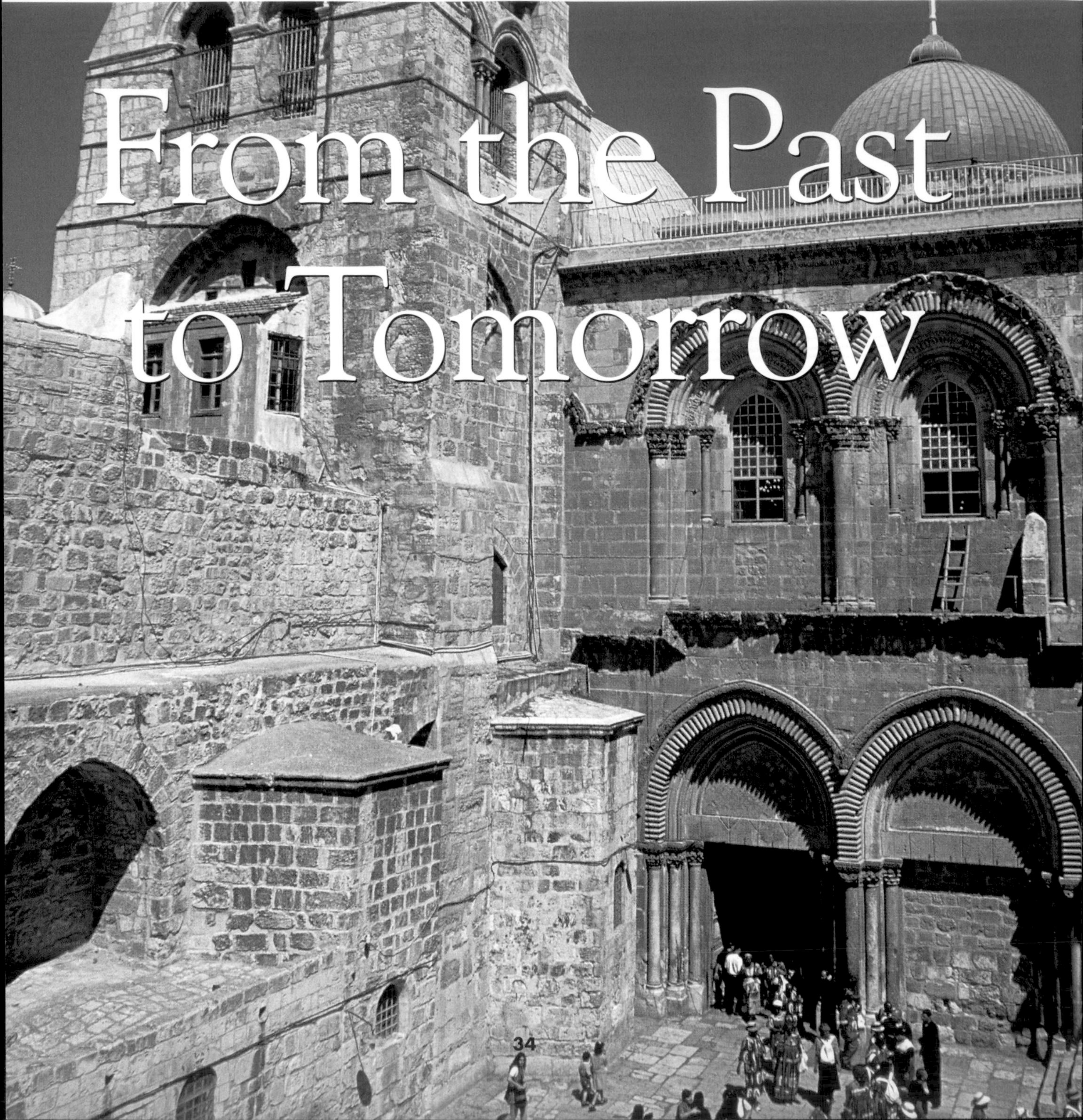

ISRAEL'S HISTORY IS CLOSELY TIED TO THAT OF THE REST of the Middle East, the area between Asia and Africa that some people call the "cradle of civilization." Palestine, Israel's name during Roman times, lay between the fertile valley of Mesopotamia to the east and the Nile Valley in Egypt to the west. Its geographic position made Palestine a crossroads for armies, refugees, nomads, and spiritual leaders.

Opposite: **The Church of the Holy Sepulchre in Jerusalem was built in the 300s.**

Many different groups have held power in what is now Israel. The British captured Jerusalem from the Ottomans in 1917.

Country Names

Philistia was an ancient country in the Middle East. The word *Philistine* was the root word for "Palestine," a term used by the Romans. The Philistines were enemies of the early Israelites. Israel is the name that God is said to have given to the biblical figure Jacob, who was one of the three fathers of the Hebrew nation. Jacob had twelve sons, whose offspring were grouped into the Twelve Tribes of Israel, or the Israelites.

The Israelites

Jericho is an ancient city. These mudbrick buildings were constructed nine thousand years ago.

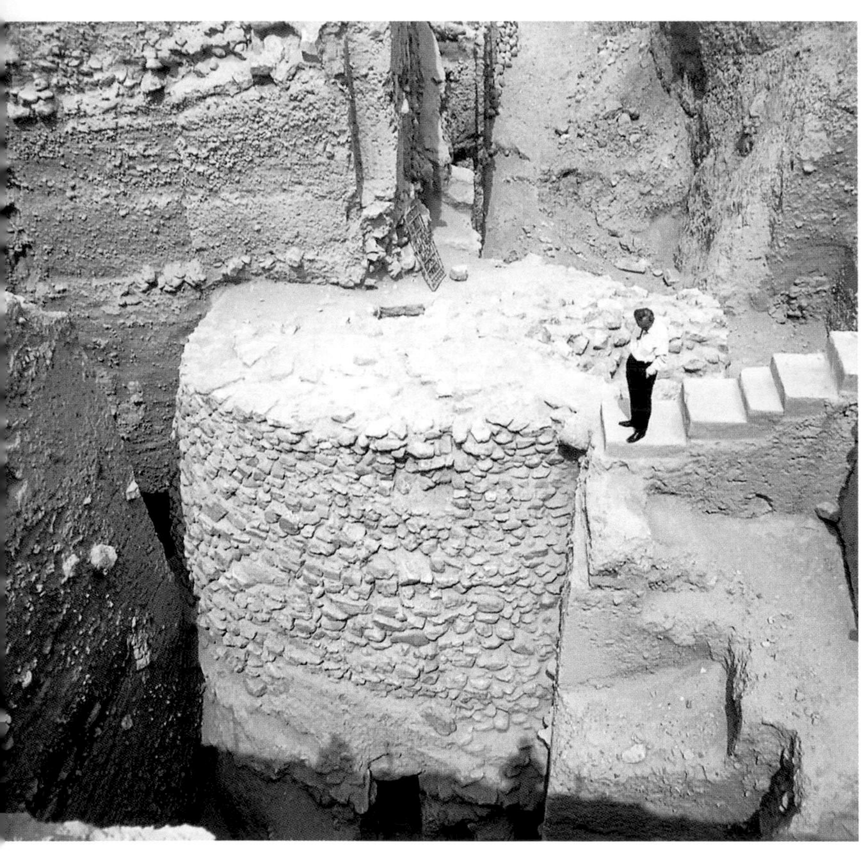

Scientists have found evidence of early humans living in caves and valleys near Jericho in what is now the West Bank—the disputed land that lies between Israel and Jordan. Jericho is one of the world's oldest cities, tracing its roots back nine thousand to eleven thousand years. Flint tools and remains of woven mats show that the people in the region were starting their long, slow march into history.

The tale of what evolved into today's Israel actually begins with Abraham, the biblical Jacob's grandfather, and other tribal leaders. Abraham is considered the founder of Judaism. A Muslim tradition says that Abraham's oldest son, Ishmael, was the father of the Arab people.

Solomon was the last king of Israel's united kingdom. He was legendary for his wisdom.

The first Israelites (residents of the ancient kingdom of Israel) probably migrated from Mesopotamia. They were a mixture of races who had fought for their survival against the Assyrians, Egyptians, Canaanites, Amorites, and Babylonians. The Israelites eventually conquered their enemies and strengthened their hold over the land. David and Solomon were two Israelite kings and great politicians described in the Bible. Under their united kingdom, from 1030 B.C. to 931 B.C., Israel was one of the major nations in the region, with its influence extending into Egypt. But over the following centuries, the Israelites were conquered by outsiders such as the Chaldeans and the Persians. The Greeks under Alexander the Great marched in next, taking power in 332 B.C.

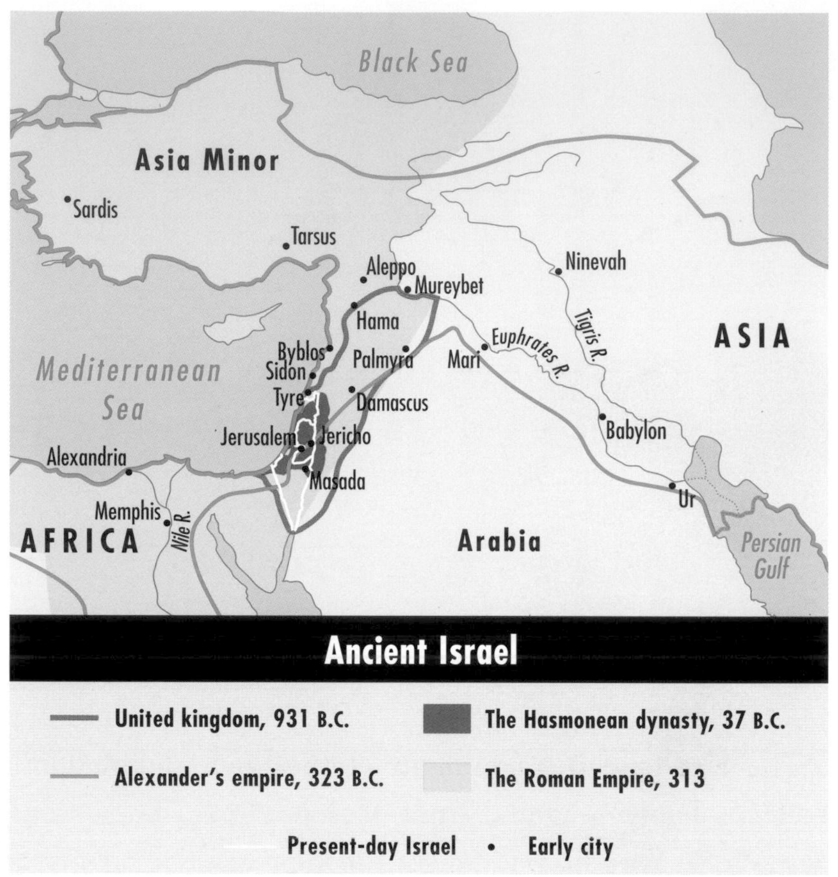

March of the Conquerors

Israel experienced a brief political revival under Judas Maccabaeus and the Hasmonean dynasty (142 B.C.–37 B.C.). But the Romans soon became the next conquerors in the region. The Roman Empire extended its reach to Palestine and the western Mediterranean by 63 B.C. The Romans ruled the countryside with an iron fist, but the Jews revolted. The rebellion was put down, and the Romans destroyed Jerusalem in A.D. 70 as punishment. A few Jews fled to the desert fortress

Emperor Titus Destroys the Temple in Jerusalem was painted by Nicolas Poussin. Jerusalem was destroyed in about A.D. 70 by the Romans.

of Masada, where they held off Roman armies for three years. In 73, the last Jewish warriors there killed their wives and children and then committed suicide rather than submit to a Roman victory.

The Diaspora

Most of the Jews who survived the Romans' destruction of Jerusalem in A.D. 70 fled the city. They spread all over the world in what is called the Diaspora, which comes from the Greek word for "scattering." The Nahum Goldmann Museum of the Jewish Diaspora at Tel Aviv University traces this dispersal of Jews. Jewish communities took root everywhere, even in such remote locales as Fiji and Haiti. No matter where they found themselves, the Jews dreamed of their own land. "The land of Israel, the blessing of its soil embraced the home of the Jew—wherever he dwelt," says a prayer that is read during the feast of Sukkot.

After the Romans destroyed Jerusalem, most of the Jews dispersed around the world in what is called the Diaspora. Only a few remained in Palestine, which eventually became part of the Byzantine Empire, or eastern Roman Empire. In 313, Emperor Constantine declared Christianity the official religion of his empire.

The Dead Sea Scrolls

In 1947, a young Bedouin named Muhammad Adh Dhib was herding his goats along the western shore of the Dead Sea, near Khirbet Qumran. He found a cave in the cliffside. Inside the cave were clay jars. One of the jars contained scrolls made of parchment and wrapped in linen. Other scrolls were found later. The writings were scriptural texts and descriptions of daily life written in Hebrew and Aramaic one hundred years before Jesus was born. They are almost the only biblical writings that have survived from that era, and they provide rich insight into the evolution of religious thought of the day. Today, these writings, known as the Dead Sea Scrolls, are displayed at the Shrine of the Book in the Israel Museum in Jerusalem.

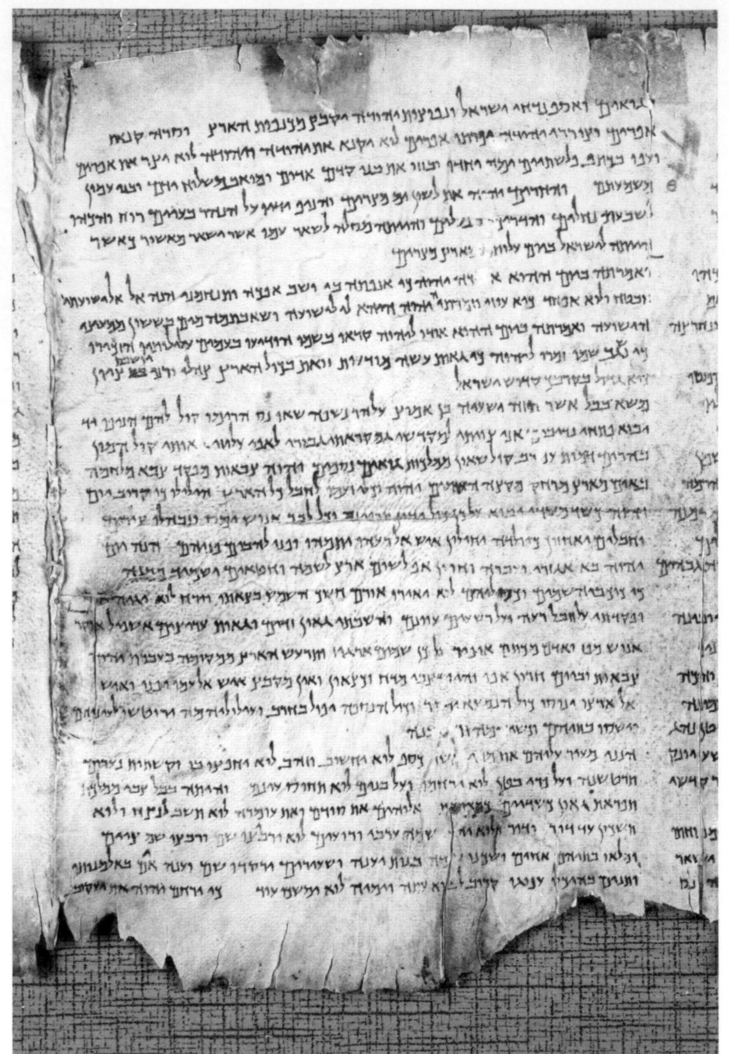

Over the next centuries, Muslims, Christian crusaders from Europe, Egyptian Mamelukes, and other conquerors swept over Palestine. In 1516, the Ottoman Turks captured Jerusalem. The Ottomans ruled Palestine from 1517 to 1917. They allowed Jews to resettle there, and by 1845 Judaism was again the most common religion in Jerusalem.

The Jews were persecuted in Russia by both citizens and police. This illustration shows Jews being assaulted in Kiev during the 1880s.

Return to Zion

A movement to resettle Palestine as a Jewish state was slowly gaining acceptance at this time. Rabbi Zvi Hirsh Kalisher (1794–1837) wrote the first book in eastern Europe backing the idea of a Jewish agricultural settlement in Palestine. British businessman Moses Montefiore (1784–1885) and French philanthropist Charles Netter (1828–1882) were among others also attempting to establish Jewish colonies there. In 1862, German-born Moses Hess (1812–1875) urged the setting up of a Jewish state in his book *Rome and Jerusalem.*

In Russia and Poland, organized massacres of Jews, called pogroms, began in the 1860s. These terrors encouraged millions of Jews to leave central Europe. Many flocked to western Europe and the Americas. Some Jews thought it would be a

The Rothschilds

One of the fathers of the Jewish homeland in Palestine was Baron Edmond de Rothschild (1845–1934). Almost single-handedly, he funded many of the small agricultural communities that were established there. He was the youngest brother of a famous financial family that traced its roots back to Frankfurt, Germany. Branches of the Rothschild financial empire were established in Austria, England, the United States, and France, as well as in Germany.

good time to "return to Zion," the Holy Land of their ancestors. They began going there toward the end of the nineteenth century, eager to start a new life. Many of their communities were supported by the Rothschilds, a banking family.

In 1881, Eliezer Ben-Yehuda moved to Palestine from Lithuania. He dedicated his life to resurrecting the Hebrew language. For centuries, Hebrew had been primarily a language of prayer. Ben-Yehuda knew that a common language would help unite the Jews who moved to Palestine. His vision prevailed, and today Hebrew is one of Israel's two national languages, along with Arabic.

The 1880s and 1890s saw a rise in anti-Jewish feeling in Europe. This caused many Jews to accept the idea of Zionism. Zionism is a movement that believes Jews have the right to return to Israel, which they consider their homeland, and that Jews should have political sovereignty in Israel.

An Austrian newspaperman named Theodor Herzl turned Zionism into a political movement. He wrote a pamphlet entitled *Der Judenstaat* (*The Jewish State*). In Hebrew, the booklet was called *Tel Aviv* (*Hill of Spring*), a name later given to a new city that would become Israel's second largest. In 1897, the first Zionist Congress gathered in Basel, Switzerland. Jews from around the world attended. The congress founded the World Zionist Organization, and Herzl became its first president.

More and more Jews moved to Palestine. They wanted to be self-sufficient, so they organized communal farms called kibbutzim (the singular form is kibbutz). The first kibbutz was founded in 1909 at Degania, near the Sea of Galilee.

Theodor Herzl was appalled by the anti-Semitism, or hatred of Jews, in European society. He became a leader of the Zionist movement.

The Kibbutz System

The kibbutz system is unique to Israel. Traditionally, all property in these communal farms was shared equally by everyone living there. The kibbutz system has changed in recent decades, and there is now more individual ownership. Kibbutz residents receive no salaries, but they are given housing and other necessities, including medical services and education.

In the past, kibbutz children lived together in a separate "children's house" away from their parents because their mothers and fathers were working all day. Children visited their parents in the afternoons and on weekends, but they always returned to the children's house to sleep. Over the years, this has changed. Youngsters now spend their days with other children, but they can sleep with their families at night.

Today, there are about 230 kibbutzim in Israel. Most modern-day kibbutzim are agricultural, but some make and sell products. Kibbutz hotels are popular vacation spots.

Britain Takes Control

During World War I (1914–1918), Great Britain tried to gain control of Palestine from the Ottoman Turks. The British and the French, who were also fighting the Ottomans, promised the Arabs they would help them establish their own homelands. A dashing British soldier, Colonel T. E. Lawrence, better known as Lawrence of Arabia, was sent to the Middle East to organize the Arabs. He molded a strong fighting force against the Ottomans. He later wrote a colorful account of the fighting in Palestine called *Seven Pillars of Wisdom*. By the war's end, Britain had defeated the Turks and captured all of Palestine.

T. E. Lawrence worked as a scientist digging up ancient ruins in the Middle East before joining the British army. His many travels there gave him great insight into the cultures of the region.

In 1917, Britain issued the Balfour Declaration. This proclamation, named after the British foreign secretary who wrote it, helped pave the way for a Jewish state. It said that the Jewish people had a right to a "national home in Palestine." This encouraged thousands of Jews to emigrate to the region after World War I.

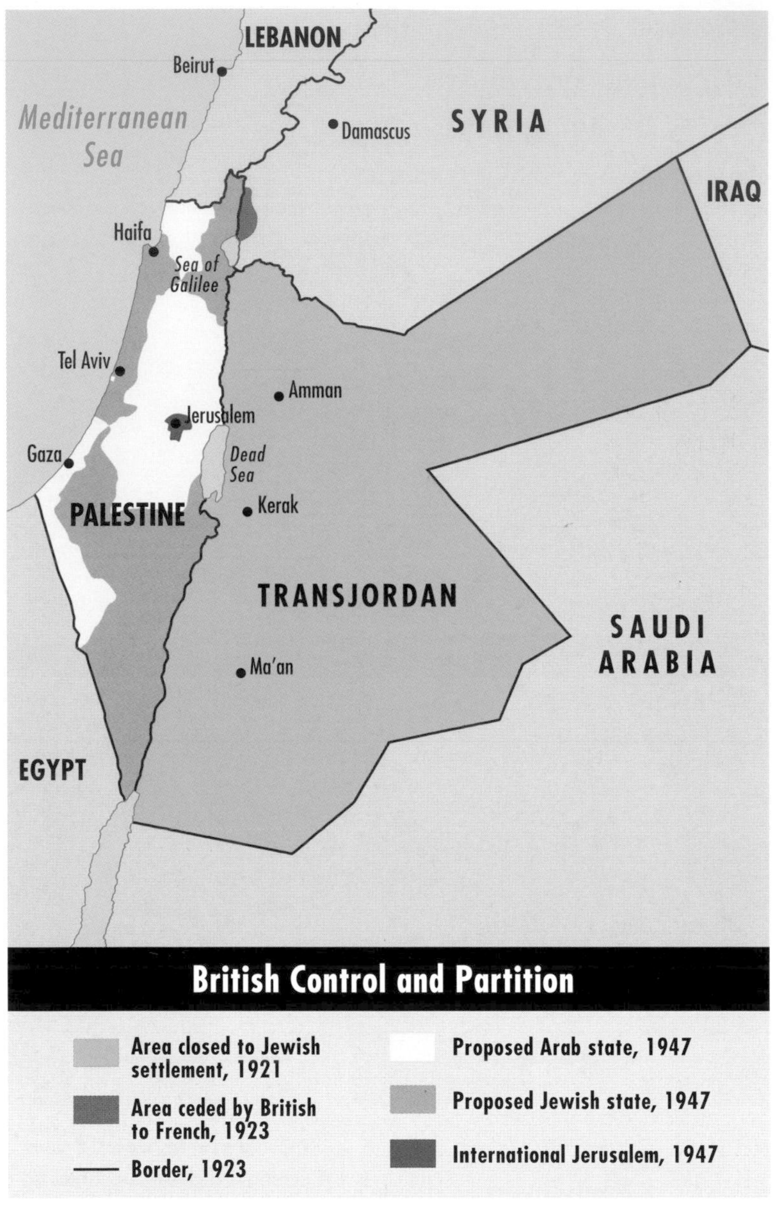

British Control and Partition

The British were now in control of Palestine—modern-day Israel and Jordan. The first British high commissioner, Sir Herbert Samuel, arrived in 1920. He was a devout Jew and an ardent Zionist who was eager to help his fellow Jews. But he leaned toward the Arabs politically, and he angered the Zionists when he later limited Jewish immigration.

In 1922, the British divided Palestine, creating the Arab Hashemite Kingdom of Transjordan east of the Jordan River. This is the present-day country of Jordan. The land to the west of the river remained "Palestine." Over the next decade, both Jews and Arabs came to Palestine, drawn to the growing prosperity there. The opening of the Hebrew University on Jerusalem's Mount Scopus in 1925 was another step taken toward the eventual creation of the State of Israel.

Rising Violence

To help Jewish newcomers, the Zionist movement created the Jewish Agency for Palestine. The organization recruited settlers, helped them find homes and jobs, and organized security for when they arrived. This was important because Arabs were fearful of the growing number of Jews. There were riots in Jerusalem, Hebron, and other communities to protest the influx of newcomers. Many Jews and Arabs died.

In 1933, Adolf Hitler and the Nazi Party came to power in Germany. Under Hitler's rule, discrimination and violence against Jews increased in Germany. More Jews moved to Palestine in hopes of finding safety. But there, the bloody riots increased. As the street battles spread, the British suggested dividing Palestine into separate Arab and Jewish states. In 1939, the British rejected the lofty ideals of the Balfour Declaration and restricted Jewish immigration into Palestine.

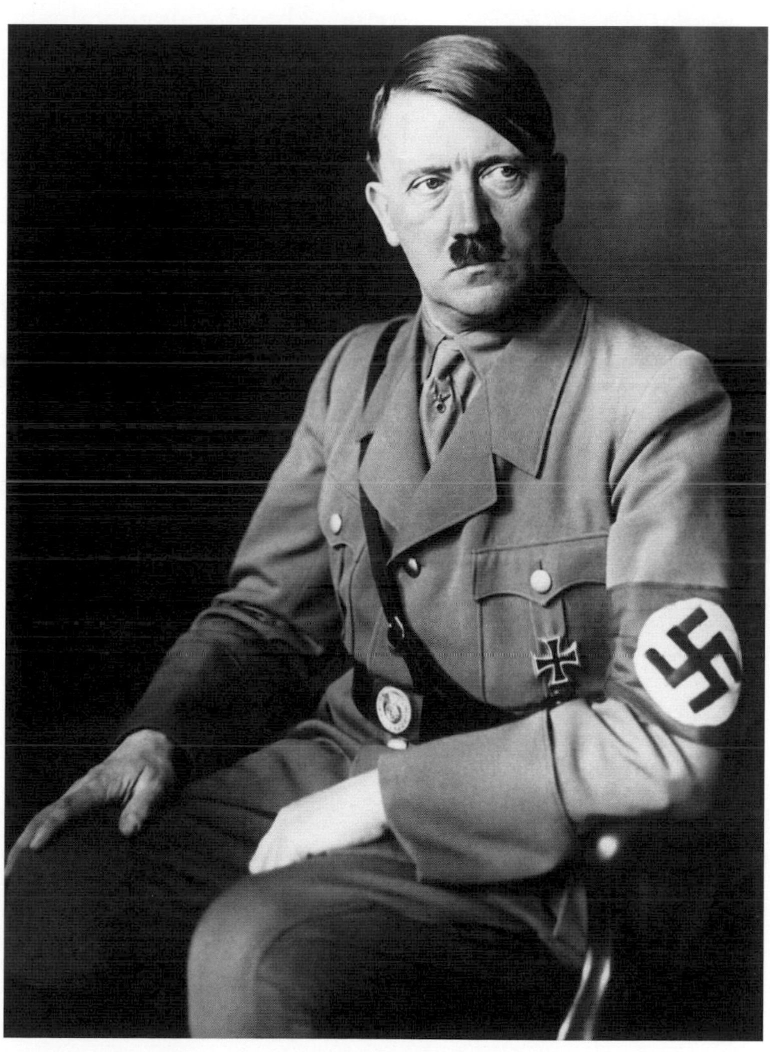

As soon as Adolf Hitler came to power, he began depriving Jews of their rights. By 1941, he had decided to systematically murder all European Jews.

These restrictions remained in effect throughout World War II (1939–1945). Even Jews attempting to escape Hitler's Nazis were prevented from entering Palestine. More than six million European Jews were eventually murdered during this time in what is known as the Holocaust. Some five thousand Jews joined the Jewish Brigade Group, a unit of the British Army. They received valuable military training, which helped them later as they began fighting for an independent state.

Toward Independence

After the war, U.S. president Harry S. Truman asked Britain to allow one hundred thousand Holocaust survivors to enter Palestine. The British refused and halted refugee ships. Thousands of Jews were interned on the Mediterranean island of Cyprus while the British tried to figure out what to do with them. Many were eventually smuggled into Palestine on leaky old ships.

Jewish refugees at a detention camp in Cyprus in 1946. Some camps in Cyprus remained open until 1949, the year after Israel was founded.

Angered by the British actions, militant Zionists attacked British troops in Palestine. In 1946, they blew up the King David Hotel, where the British army command and government officials were housed. Ninety-one people, including forty-one Arabs and seventeen Jews, were killed in the blast.

Britain soon announced that it was going to withdraw from Palestine. In 1947, the British asked the United Nations (UN)—an organization formed in the aftermath of World War II to promote world peace—to seek a solution to the region's political woes. On November 29, the UN passed a resolution splitting Palestine into Jewish and Arab states. The Arabs rejected the plan, and war broke out. Despite the fighting, the independent State of Israel was announced on May 14, 1948. Israel was immediately invaded by Iraq, Syria, Egypt, Jordan, and Lebanon, but the Israelis beat back their enemies.

In 1949, Israel signed armistice agreements with Syria, Egypt, Jordan, and Lebanon. To separate the warring parties, Jerusalem was divided. Israel remained in control of Jerusalem's western section, while Jordan took the eastern part. A period of relative calm followed in which Israel's economy mushroomed and its population doubled.

Frequent Warfare

The calm didn't last for long. By the mid-1950s, Palestinian militants supported by Egypt were making frequent raids into Israel. Then Egypt blocked Israeli ships from using the Suez Canal, which connects the Mediterranean Sea and the Red Sea. The Egyptians also stopped Israeli ships from entering the Gulf of Aqaba. In response, Israel attacked Egypt in 1956. Before long, the UN ended the fighting and sent in peacekeeping troops.

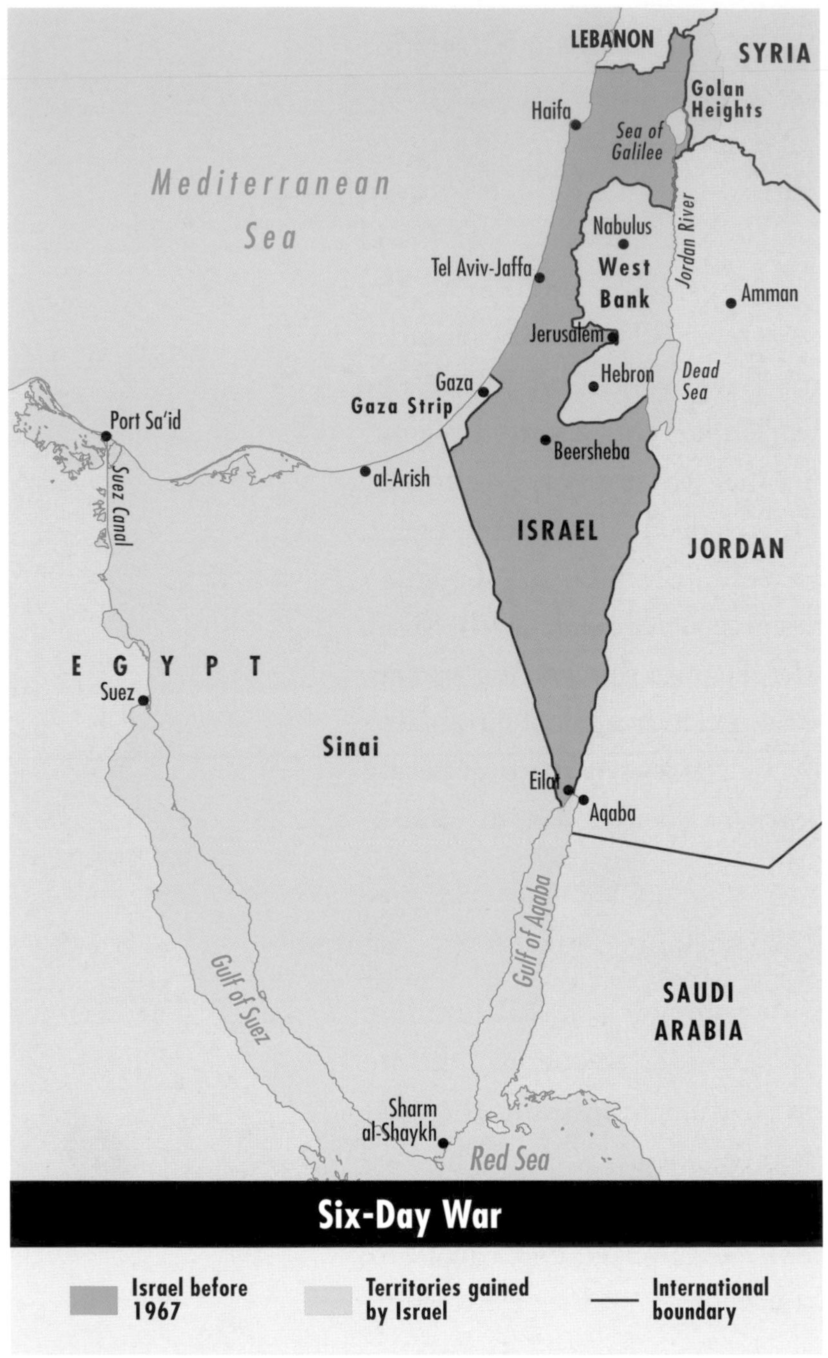

In 1967, when the UN peacekeepers left, Egypt sent soldiers into the Sinai and blocked access to the Israeli port of Eilat. On June 5, 1967, Israel attacked Egypt. That same day, Israel attacked Syria. Jordan soon joined Egypt and Syria in fighting Israel, but the Arab states were quickly defeated. This "Six-Day War" resulted in a reunited Jerusalem. The Israelis took over the Gaza Strip, the Sinai, and the Golan Heights and occupied the West Bank. This enraged the Arab League, a group of Arab countries, which vowed no peace with Israel.

Israel was constantly on the alert. There were plane hijackings and a massacre of Israeli athletes at the 1972 Olympic

Menachem Begin (left) shakes hands with Anwar el-Sadat while President Jimmy Carter looks on. Their talks at Camp David led to a peace treaty between Egypt and Israel.

Games in Munich, West Germany. On the Jewish holiday of Yom Kippur in 1973, Egypt and Syria attacked Israel along the Suez Canal and the Golan Heights. But Israel was able to push back the Egyptians and Syrians.

Moves toward Peace

Over time, tensions between the Israelis and the Egyptians eased. Egyptian leader Anwar el-Sadat and Israeli prime minister Menachem Begin began peace talks. In 1978, the two men met with U.S. president Jimmy Carter at Camp David in the United States. The result was the Camp David Accords, which led to a peace treaty between the countries the following year. Begin and Sadat received the Nobel Peace Prize in 1978 for their efforts at bringing peace to the Middle East.

In 1982, Israel pulled out of the Sinai. The same year, however, Israel invaded Lebanon to protect its northern settlements from Palestinian attacks. The UN stepped in to replace Israeli troops in Lebanon. By 1985, the only Israeli presence there was along a security strip between the two countries.

In 1987, an *intifada* (an Arabic word meaning "uprising" or "shaking off") began. This was a violent protest by Palestinians against Israel's military occupation of the Gaza Strip and the West Bank. Rocks thrown at Israeli soldiers soon escalated to bombs and bullets. Dozens of people were killed. The intifada influenced Israeli elections, affected the economy, and made Israelis worry about their security.

Israel has suffered frequent bombings in recent years. In 2002, a Palestinian suicide bomber blew up a bus in Jerusalem, killing twenty people.

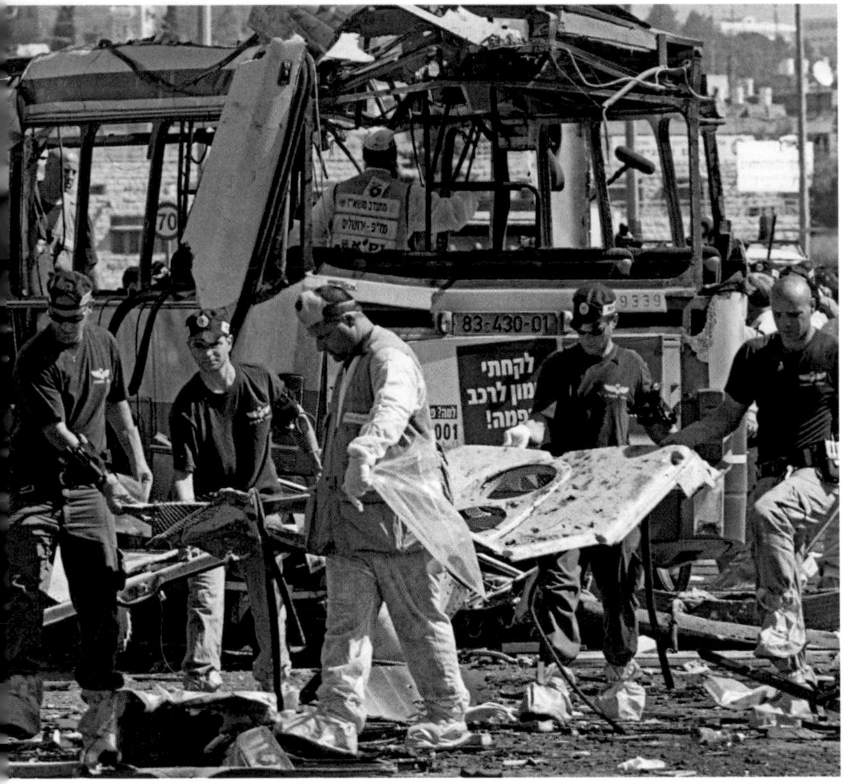

Steps Forward

In 1993, the Israeli government and the Palestine Liberation Organization—a political and military organization representing the Palestinians—agreed to the Oslo Accords, officially called the Declaration of Principles. After long days of talks at Camp David, President Bill Clinton hosted Israeli prime minister Yitzhak Rabin

President Bill Clinton encourages Yitzhak Rabin (left) and Yasir Arafat to shake hands. Though they had agreed on a peace deal, strife would continue.

and Palestinian leader Yasir Arafat at the White House, where the Declaration of Principles was signed. On September 13, 1993, the world's photographers recorded a historic handshake between Rabin and Arafat. The greeting between the two set off a positive chain of events in the Middle East. Jordan and Israel signed a peace treaty on October 26, 1994. The Syrians, who had long supported the Palestinian cause, also launched talks with Israeli officials.

But terrorist attacks by Palestinian extremists continued in Jerusalem and Tel Aviv into the 2000s. Efforts were made to restart negotiations. In 2003, Israeli prime minister Ariel Sharon surprised the world by saying he expected to pull Israeli soldiers and settlers out of the Gaza Strip. In 2005, he did just that. It is hoped that this may put the peace process back on track. The world is watching and waiting.

CHAPTER FIVE

Birthing a New Nation

Israel was proclaimed a state at 4:00 p.m. on May 14, 1948, during a ceremony in Tel Aviv that drew cheering crowds. The declaration became effective the next day as the last British troops left the country. But not everyone was elated. Palestinian Arabs remember May 15 as *al-Nakba*, or "the catastrophe."

Opposite: **David Ben-Gurion (left) signs a document establishing Israel as an independent state.**

The U.S. and British governments had wanted David Ben-Gurion, the head of the World Zionist Organization, to delay the announcement of the new country for another six months. They were worried about continuing warfare in the region and did not want to stir up Palestinian nationalism. Nor did they want to become directly involved in a conflict there.

Yet Ben-Gurion knew that timing was important. His military advisers told him that his new state would have only a 50 percent chance of surviving impending attacks by its Arab neighbors. The Jews had waited for this moment for 1,878 years, ever since their ancestors had been expelled from ancient Israel by the Romans. In the spring of 1948, an eager Ben-Gurion chose a site for announcing Israel's independence. The location of the thirty-two-minute ceremony was kept secret until the last minute for fear of sabotage.

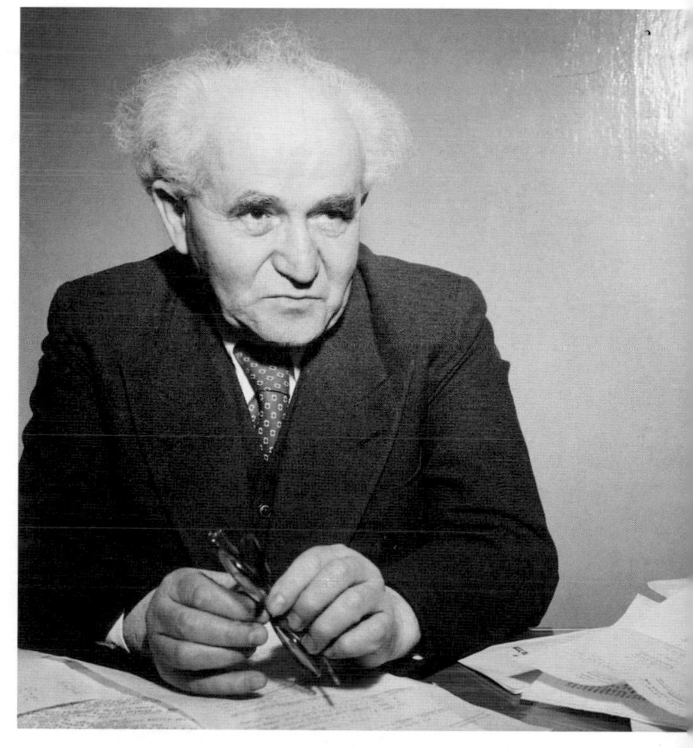

A committed Zionist, David Ben-Gurion moved from Poland to Palestine at age nineteen. In 1948, he become Israel's first prime minister.

Ben-Gurion selected a building built in 1911 that had been the home of Meir Dizengoff, Tel Aviv's first mayor. In 1936, the house had been enlarged to become the city's art museum. Still, the building was not quite prepared for the birth of a nation. Chairs were borrowed from a coffeehouse, carpets from a carpet store, and a microphone from a nearby shop. A portrait of Theodor Herzl, founder of the Zionist movement, hung on a wall. On both sides of the picture were new Israeli flags.

The room was ready, yet there remained one challenge. What would the new country be named? Some politicians wanted to call it "Zion." Others wanted "Judea." Still others thought "State of the Jews" was best. But the majority chose *Medinat Yisrael*, the "State of Israel." The dispute was resolved barely thirty minutes before the ceremony was to begin.

Thousands of people crowded Rothschild Boulevard in downtown Tel Aviv to witness history in the making. After the dignitaries were seated, Ben-Gurion described Israel's

The Israeli Flag

Israel's national flag is white with a blue six-pointed star called the Shield of David centered between two horizontal blue bands. According to Jewish tradition, David, king of the ancient Israelites, carried this six-pointed star on his shield. This flag, which had been the flag of the Zionist movement, became the official Israeli flag six months after independence.

goals and dreams as an independent country and its desire for peace with the Arabs. He concluded by saying, "*Zot Medinat Yisrael*" ("This is the State of Israel"). Tel Aviv's chief rabbi then recited a prayer thanking God, who "brought us to this moment." On that uplifting note, Israel greeted the world.

Israel's Government

Israel has a one-house legislature called the Knesset. The 120 members of the Knesset are elected by voters to four-year terms. The Knesset passes legislation, helps form national policy, works out budgets, debates issues, elects the president, and keeps an eye on cabinet members. The Knesset has eleven permanent committees that deal with topics ranging from foreign affairs to education.

The president is the head of state in Israel, an important ceremonial position. The president signs treaties and laws enacted by the

Israel's National Anthem

"Hatikvah" ("The Hope"), the national anthem of Israel, was written as a poem by Naphtali Herz Imber in 1878. Samuel Cohen set the poem to music a few years later, basing the tune on an old folk song.

As long as deep in the heart
The soul of a Jew yearns,
And towards the East
An eye looks to Zion,
Our hope is not yet lost,
The hope of two thousand years,
To be a free people in our land,
The land of Zion and Jerusalem.

The president of Israel is elected by the members of the Knesset. Moshe Katsav was elected president in 2000.

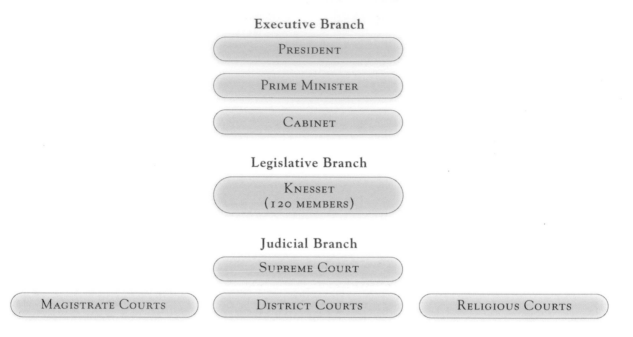

NATIONAL GOVERNMENT OF ISRAEL

Executive Branch

PRESIDENT

PRIME MINISTER

CABINET

Legislative Branch

KNESSET
(120 MEMBERS)

Judicial Branch

SUPREME COURT

MAGISTRATE COURTS | DISTRICT COURTS | RELIGIOUS COURTS

Knesset and appoints diplomats, judges, and the governor of the Bank of Israel. The president is elected to a seven-year term and cannot serve more than two terms. Moshe Katsav became the country's eighth president in 2000. Born in Iran, he immigrated to Israel with his family in 1951. He is the first Israeli president born in a Muslim country.

The prime minister, elected by the people of Israel, is head of Israel's government as well as head of the cabinet. The cabinet is the top policymaking body in Israel. It is usually made up of members of several parties. The cabinet introduces legislation, which Knesset members vote upon after it has been revised by Knesset committees.

Golda Meir

Women have long played a major role in Israel's government. One of the most important was Prime Minister Golda Meir (1898–1978). Meir was born in Kiev, Russia, in 1898. She was raised in Milwaukee, Wisconsin, and then moved to Palestine in the 1920s. Long active in politics, Meir became prime minister in 1969. She left office in 1974, following criticism of her handling of Israel's 1973 war against Egypt and Syria. She died in 1978.

Israel's two largest parties are the Labor Party and the Likud Party. There are several smaller parties, including those with strong religious leanings such as the Flag of Torah and United Israel. Traditionally, most Arab Israelis have voted for the Labor Party or such nationalist groups as the United Arab List. A prime minister's strength is determined by the amount of support received by these various parties. A government can be replaced if the parties object to a prime minister's policies.

A Prime Minister's Murder

Prime Minister Yitzhak Rabin continued to pursue peace with Israel's Arab neighbors years after shaking hands with Yasir Arafat at the White House. Some conservative Israelis objected to this. They did not want to compromise on giving up land that they felt was historically theirs to people they considered enemies. Rabin was assassinated on November 4, 1995, by an Israeli who opposed the peace process. A memorial in Tel Aviv marks the spot where Rabin was killed.

The Court System

The Supreme Court building is in Jerusalem. The justices both hear appeals from lower courts and review the actions of other parts of the government.

Israelis turn to their court system for help. The Supreme Court, the nation's highest court, is seen as guarding the values of freedom and justice. Supreme Court rulings are binding—the last word in any dispute. The court usually consists of three judges, but up to eleven can serve. The justices are appointed by the president and serve for life.

The Israeli judicial system includes criminal courts, civil courts, and military courts. There are also special courts for traffic, insurance, juvenile, and labor issues.

Personal matters such as marriage and divorce are

handled in religious courts. There are separate courts for Jews, Muslims, Christians, and Druze.

Local Government

Israel is divided into six administrative districts called *mehozot.* (The singular form is *mehoz.*) The mehozot are managed by district commissioners. Fourteen subdistricts are coordinated by district officers. These officials are appointed by the minister of the interior. They draft local legislation, set tax rates and budgets, and approve public works projects. Mayors and members of municipal councils are also elected.

A Strong Military

Some visitors to Israel are surprised to see the numbers of young people in military uniform on the streets. Israel is in a state of constant military preparedness because of the potential for terrorist attacks. Soldiers laden with packs and automatic weapons hitchhike from designated stops along the main highways.

Everyone over the age of eighteen must serve in the military, except students attending religious schools. Men serve three years. Unmarried women serve twenty-one months and generally do not serve in combat roles. Even before Israel was a state, women guarded outposts and served in military units. Many female Israeli soldiers are instructors, teaching everything from sniping to tank maneuvers. Others help teach immigrant recruits from countries such as Ethiopia, Canada, India, England, France, and Morocco to speak, read, and write Hebrew.

A Jewish settlement in Gaza. In September 2005, Israel withdrew from Gaza, and the settlements were evacuated.

Leaving Gaza

The Gaza Strip is a 139-square-mile (360 sq-km) area of sand and boulders that was not included as part of Israel in the peace treaty of 1949. It has been the home of Palestinian refugees who fled Israel when it became an independent nation. The area was under Egyptian and United Nations control over the years until Israel took control of it after the Six-Day War. In 1994, the Gaza Strip, which is home to almost 1.4 million Palestinians, came under limited Palestinian control.

In 2005, however, almost nine thousand Israeli settlers were also living in the Gaza Strip. Some were secular, or non-religious, Israelis who had moved in search of bigger homes and a pleasant view of the Mediterranean. They set up factories, hothouses for growing flowers, and other business. Others were militantly religious. They believed that God had promised the land to Jews and that it was a sin to give it up. To many Israelis, the Jewish settlers were radicals stirring up trouble.

The settlers were also a problem for Prime Minister Ariel Sharon. The Israeli government felt the presence of the settlers endangered the start of a peace process with Mahmoud Abbas, the newly elected president of the Palestinian Authority. There were also concerns that Israel would have a difficult time remaining a democratic Jewish state while controlling a region with such a large Arab population. After earlier supporting the settlements, Sharon decided to give full control of the Gaza Strip to Palestinians. By September 2005, the Israeli army withdrew, and Jewish settlers were relocated.

Competing Claims

Israel still claims large areas of the West Bank of the Jordan River and the entire city of Jerusalem. The West Bank is located west of the Jordan River. Israel lies to the west, north, and south, while the country of Jordan is to the east. In biblical times, this region was known as Judea and Samaria. Today, about 40 percent of the West Bank is under the jurisdiction of the Palestinian Authority. Israel controls the Israeli settlements there, plus rural and border regions.

Palestinians want stretches along the Jordan River and part of Jerusalem to be under Palestinian control. If Palestine became a nation, the Palestinians would claim Jerusalem as its capital. Israel, however, views the whole of Jerusalem as its capital. Most Israelis oppose the surrender of territories that were historically Jewish, such as Judea and Samaria. An ongoing peace process between Palestinians and Israelis is attempting to reconcile all these claims.

In 2003, Israel began building a 425-mile (684 km) barricade separating the West Bank from the rest of Israel. The barrier was designed to keep terrorists from infiltrating Israel. In 2004, the International Court of Justice, the United Nations' highest legal body, issued an opinion that the fence was contrary to international law. But many Israelis consider it a success.

Jerusalem: Did You Know This?

Jerusalem has been settled almost continuously for more than three thousand years, though under different names. It was made the capital of modern Israel in 1950. Today, it is home to about 680,000 people.

Jerusalem is located on two rocky hills. The Old City, which is surrounded by walls, is made up of four neighborhoods: Jewish, Christian, Armenian, and Muslim. Each has a maze of narrow streets lined with tiny shops. Outside these ancient walls is "new" Jerusalem, which sprawls out into the hills.

The city contains important Jewish, Christian, and Muslim holy sites. Each religious community has places of interest. The Greek Orthodox Museum lies in the Christian quarter of the Old City. The Islamic Museum

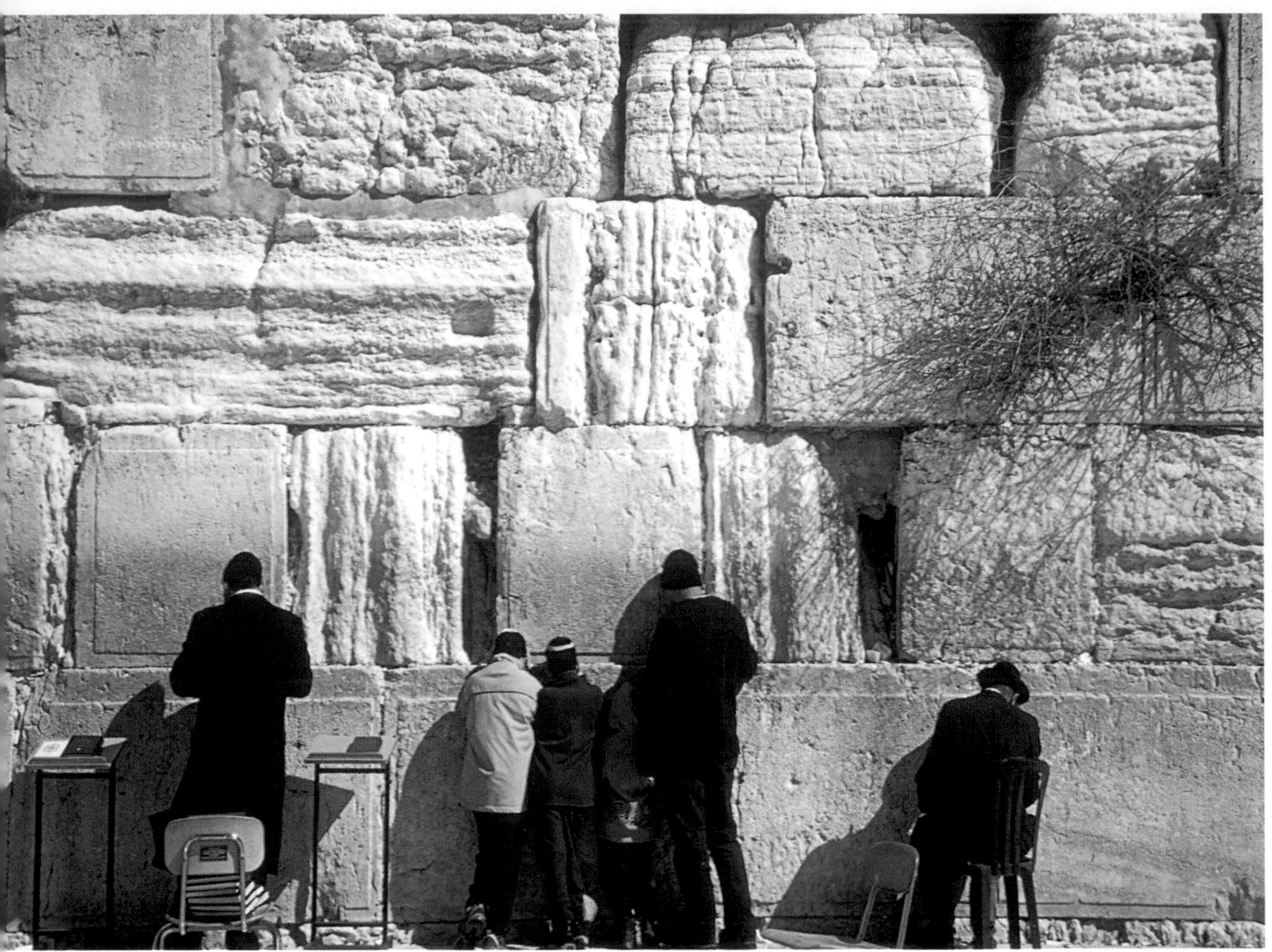

of the Temple Mount depicts Islam's culture and heritage. The Wailing Wall, or the Western Wall of the old temple (left), is one of the Jewish world's most holy shrines. It dates from 20 B.C.

The Israel Museum in Jerusalem is Israel's largest museum and a leading cultural institution. It has four wings covering periods and world cultures from ancient through modern times. Rare artifacts include the Dead Sea Scrolls. The Rockefeller Archaeological Museum is a landmark building in East Jerusalem that houses a huge collection of ancient artifacts found throughout Palestine when it was governed by the British between 1920 and 1948.

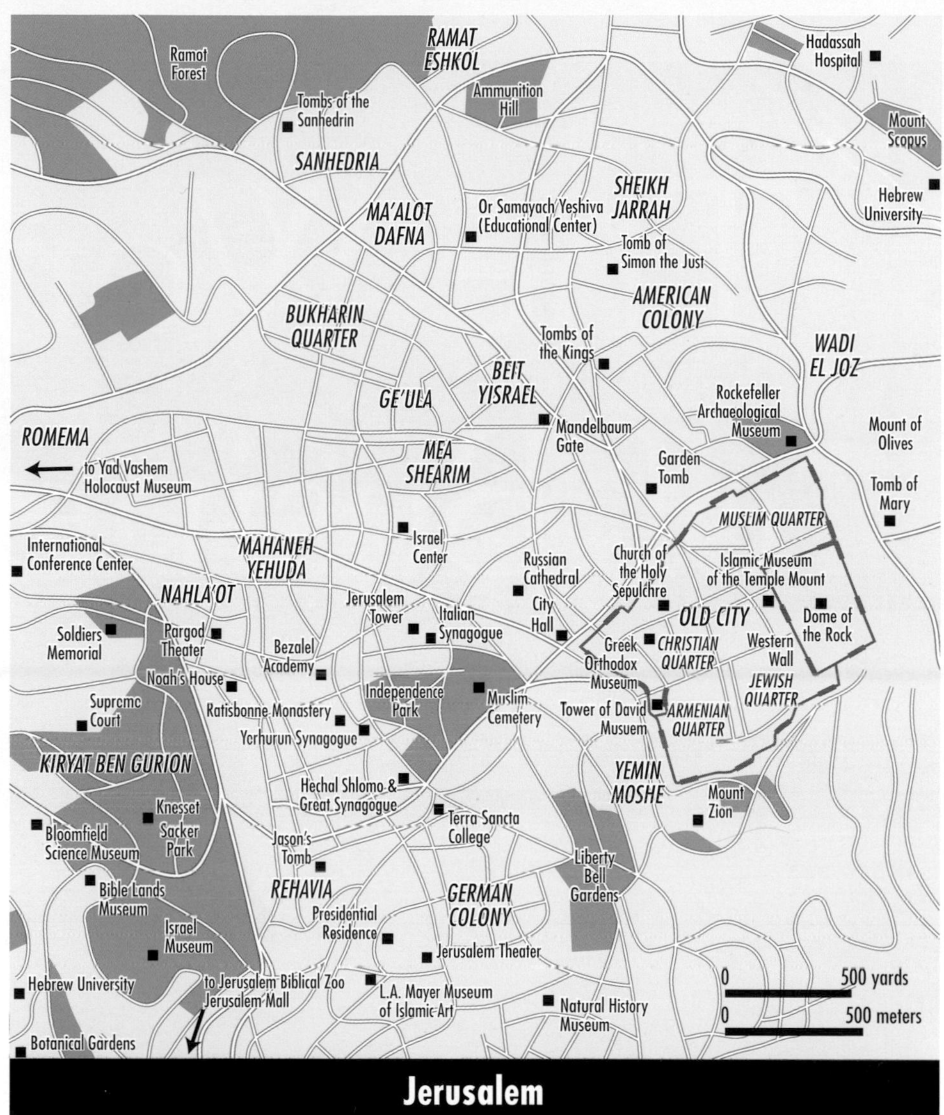

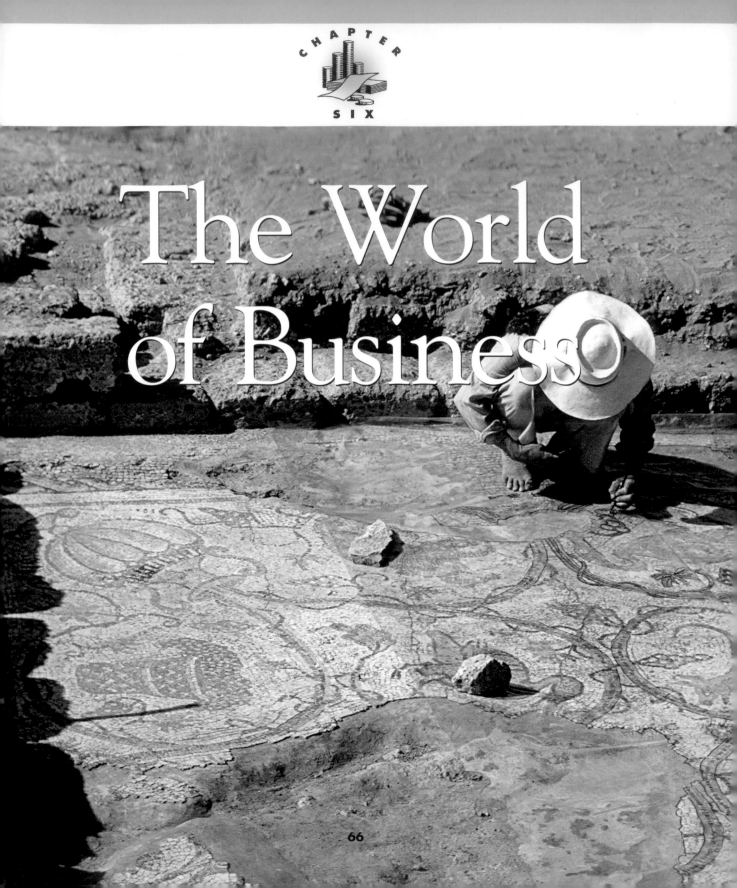

The World of Business

Israel's high-tech industries have boomed in recent years.

Israel is a hardworking country with about two million skilled employees. Almost 75 percent of workers have service jobs. Economic bustle is everywhere, from the Weizmann Institute of Science in Rehovot, south of Tel Aviv, where semiconductor crystals are made, to the Su-Pad Company in Rosh Ha'Ayin, where plastic products are made. In the past twenty years, Israel's high-techology industries have grown quickly. Computer industries are doing so well and have attracted so much international interest that Israel is nicknamed "the Second Silicon Valley," after the area in California where many computer products are made. Israeli research and development can take credit for many technologies, such as instant messaging.

Opposite: **A scientist cleans an ancient floor at Caesara, a city built two thousand years ago.**

What Israel Grows, Makes, and Mines

Agriculture (2002)	
Poultry	453,390 metric tons
Cheese	104,252 metric tons
Beef, veal	64,362 metric tons
Mining (2003)	
Phosphate rock	3,500,000 metric tons
Potash	1,930,000 metric tons
Manufacturing	
Cement (2003)	7,000,000 metric tons
Cardboard and paper (2003)	95,000 metric tons
Pulp fiber (2002)	15,000 metric tons

Farming

The first settlers in Palestine worked hard turning the barren landscape into an oasis of flowering beauty. But with the growth of cities and expanding industries, agriculture has stepped into the background of the Israeli economy.

Today, only 4 percent of the labor force works in agriculture. During peak planting and harvesting time, seasonal workers from eastern Europe, Thailand, and other Asian countries are brought in to help. Poultry, dairy products, beef, vegetables, cotton, citrus, and other fruits are all produced in Israel. Except for some grains, Israel is self-sufficient in its food production. It exports citrus fruits and other products around the world. Many of the oranges, melons, kiwis, and mangoes seen in Europe, Canada, and the United States come from Israel. Long-stemmed roses, carnations, and other flowers are

From Chile to Israel

Some unusual farm animals live in Israel today. Ilan Dvir has the only alpaca ranch in the Middle East. He raises alpacas brought from Chile in 1990 to his ranch in the Negev Desert. Alpacas are llama-like creatures. They are raised for their fine wool, which is sold to tourists who drop by to admire the herd of more than six hundred animals.

also grown year-round in greenhouses and sold in Europe. They make up about a quarter of Israel's agricultural exports.

Cattle are among Israel's leading agricultural products. There are 340,000 cattle in the country.

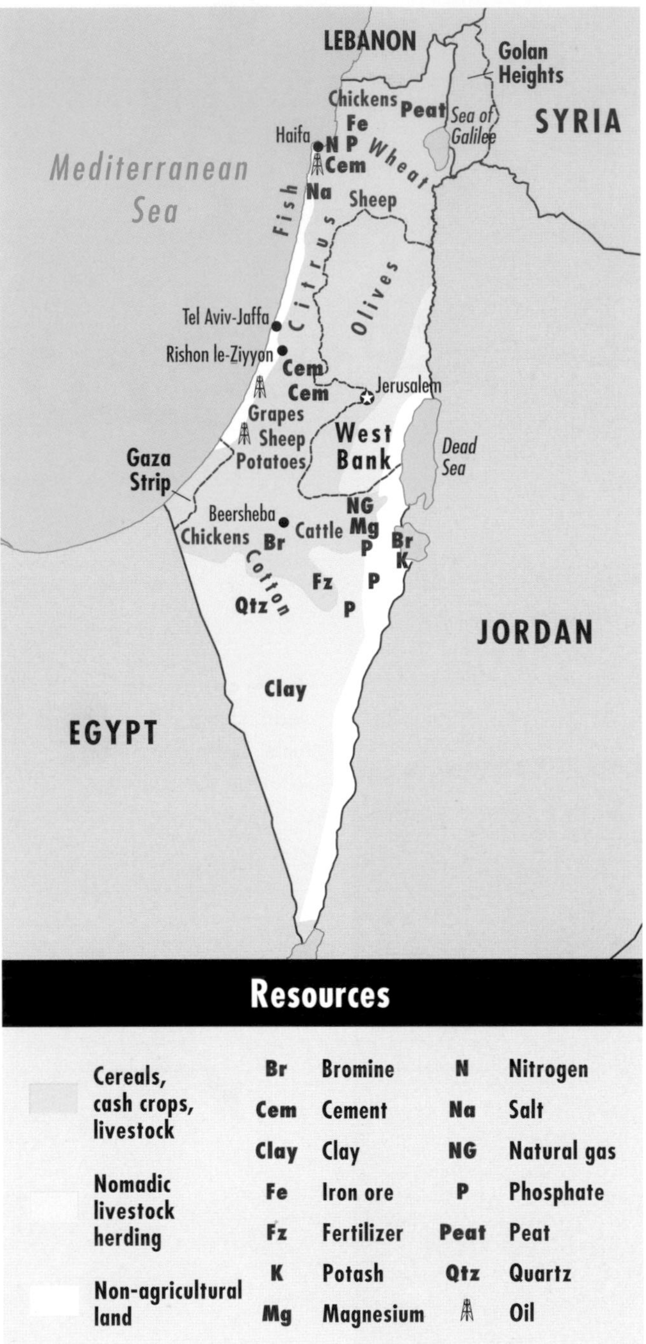

The Rich Golan

The Golan Heights was a battlefield in 1967. Today, tractors chug across the rich landscape where tanks once roared. The Golan shows astounding agricultural development. Apricots, nectarines, grapefruits, plums, bananas, avocados, dates, and mangoes are grown in the south. To the north, farmers cultivate cherries, apples, blueberries, and pears. Most of the fruit consumed in Israel is provided by these farms. The main field crops in the Golan include corn, onions, tomatoes, and cotton. Israeli farmers also raise potatoes. These are turned into tons of french fries that are served at restaurants across Israel, including more than eighty McDonald's. Cows and sheep graze on the pastures of the Golan, while turkeys and chickens are raised in pens. Poultry consumption in Israel is among the highest in the world.

The Water Question

The major water sources in Israel are the narrow Jordan River, the Sea of

Galilee, and a few smaller rivers. There are no large freshwater lakes or long rivers in Israel, although it does have some underground lakes. Each year, Israel receives an average of only 28 inches (71 cm) of rain in the north and 2 inches (5 cm) in the south. This presents a problem for agriculture, making it necessary to use the precious water for crop irrigation. An intricate system of pipes, tunnels, dams, pumping stations, canals, and reservoirs brings water from the northern and central regions to the arid south.

Much of Israel gets little rainfall, so farmers must use irrigation equipment to water their crops.

Foreign Aid

Israel is the largest recipient of U.S. foreign aid. Grants, loans, and other forms of financial assistance total in the billions of dollars for military, education, and other projects. In addition to this government money, foreign supporters who believe that there needs to be a homeland for the Jewish people also send money to help build museums, hospitals, swimming pools, and other facilities, as well as to help with university programs, religious studies, and other humanitarian purposes.

For irrigation to be possible, Israelis have to be efficient and conserve what little water there is. They regularly recycle wastewater and take the salt out of seawater. Israel also imports crops that need lots of water from other countries and cultivates crops that need less water.

Water is a constant source of conflict in the Middle East. For centuries, nations have argued and fought over control of the Jordan River. However, they are slowly learning to work together. Since signing a peace treaty in the early 1990s, Israel and Jordan have viewed water as a shared resource. Because both face shortages, they realize that they needed to cooperate on water-storage projects and to establish antipollution policies to improve water quality.

Still, Israel's limited water supply remains a concern. Agriculture uses almost four-fifths of the nation's water supply. Should the country import more food so that less water is used for agriculture? This would save more water for industry. But how much industry can Israel support?

Industry

Diamond cutting and polishing, high-tech electronics, textiles, apparel, and chemical products are among Israel's leading industries. The manufacturing of military and transport equipment, computer technology, metal products, and electrical equipment adds up to economic success. The more recently developed Golan Heights area adds an edge to the economy because of new industries sprouting up there in plastics, electro-optics, defense systems, dairy products, chemicals, telecommunications, computer hardware, food packaging, shoes, and research and development. Mining is big along the Dead Sea shores, yielding a treasure of potash, magnesium chloride, and bromine. There is so much mining there that it is affecting the depth of the water.

A technician inspects computer parts. High-technology equipment is among the country's leading exports.

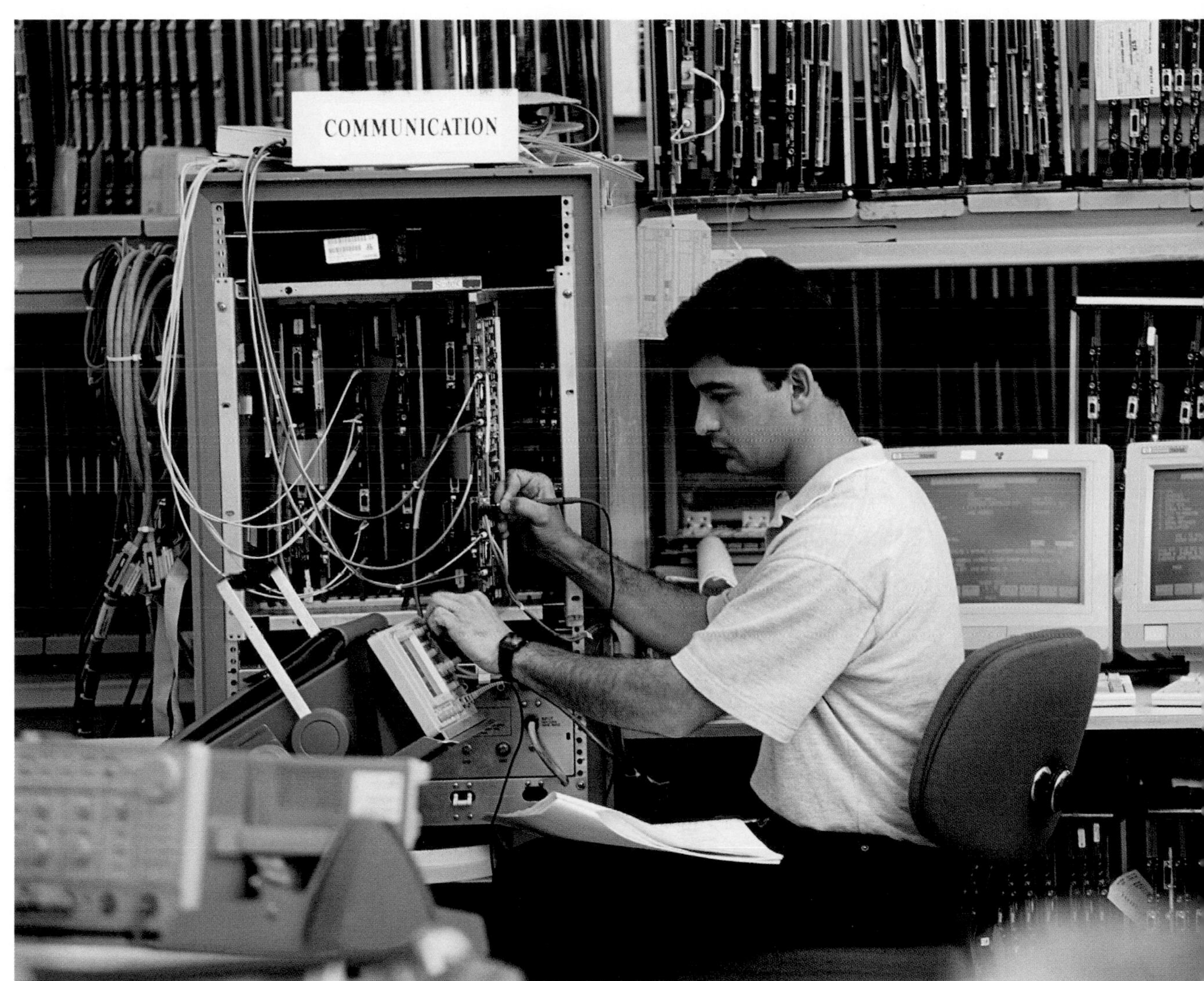

Tourism

Tourism is one of Israel's top industries. It brings in hundreds of millions of dollars annually. But tourism has been declining since 2000, when hostilities between the Israelis and the Palestinians intensified.

Many people travel to Israel to visit ancient sites and enjoy the pleasant climate. Hiking is a popular activity at Timna Valley National Park.

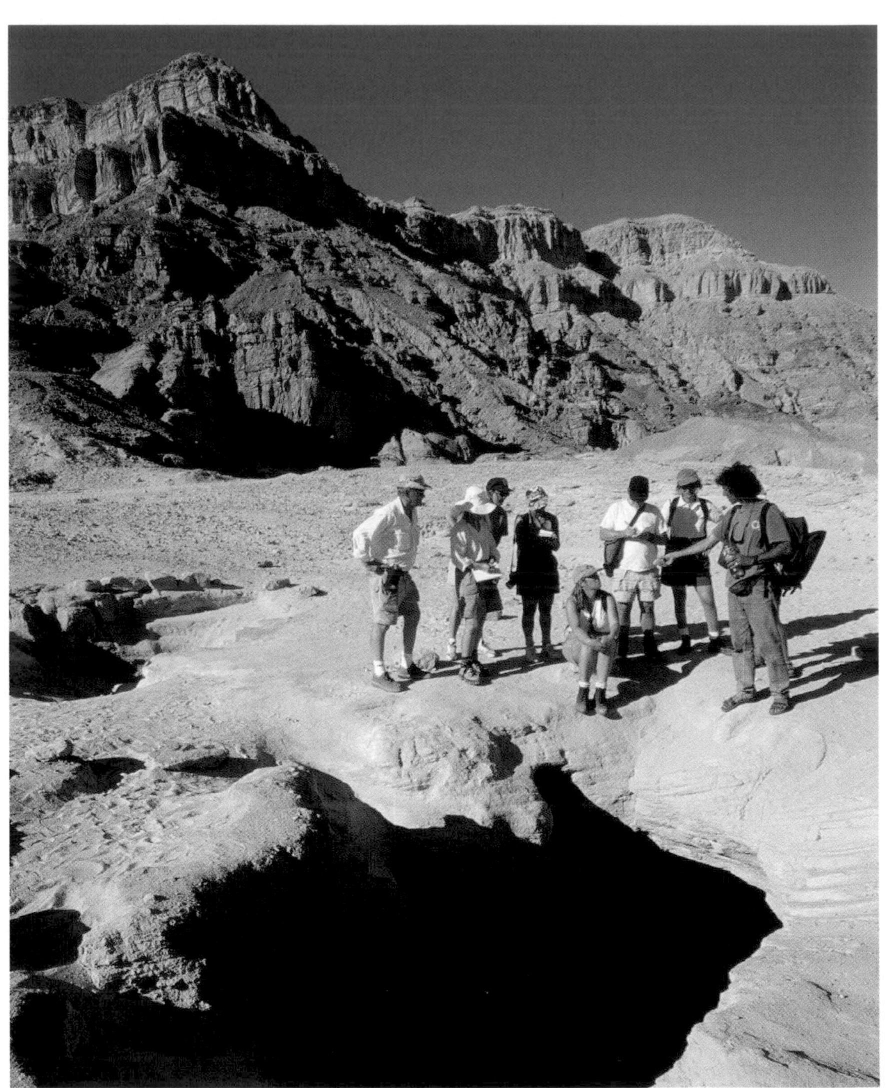

Currency Facts

Israel's official currency is the Israeli new shekel. A shekel is divided into one hundred agorot. In 2005, 1 U.S. dollar was equal to 4.5 shekels. Banknotes come in denominations of 20, 50, 100, and 200 shekels. There are 1-, 5-, and 10-shekel coins as well as 5-, 10-, and 50-agorot coins.

The front of the 20-shekel bill features a picture of Moshe Sharett, Israel's second prime minister, along with the Israeli flag and a high school. The 50-shekel note has a picture of writer Shmuel Yosef Agnon, backed by books and buildings. The 100-shekel note shows a portrait of Yitzhak Ben-Zvi, Israel's second president, backed by a village and a group of people. The 200-shekel note has a portrait of scholar and politician Zalman Shazar and a drawing of elementary school students.

Every year, about 1.2 million visitors travel to Israel. History attracts some visitors. Other visitors are religious pilgrims. Muslims, Christians, and Jews visit sites that are sacred in their religions. Still others come for the culture and sunny climate. The Dead Sea region has been a popular resort area since ancient times. Its year-round sunshine and clean air and the healing properties of its mineral-rich waters continue to draw visitors from around the world. People say the mineral-rich mud can cure skin ailments. Some spas offer special beauty packages with massages and mud packs.

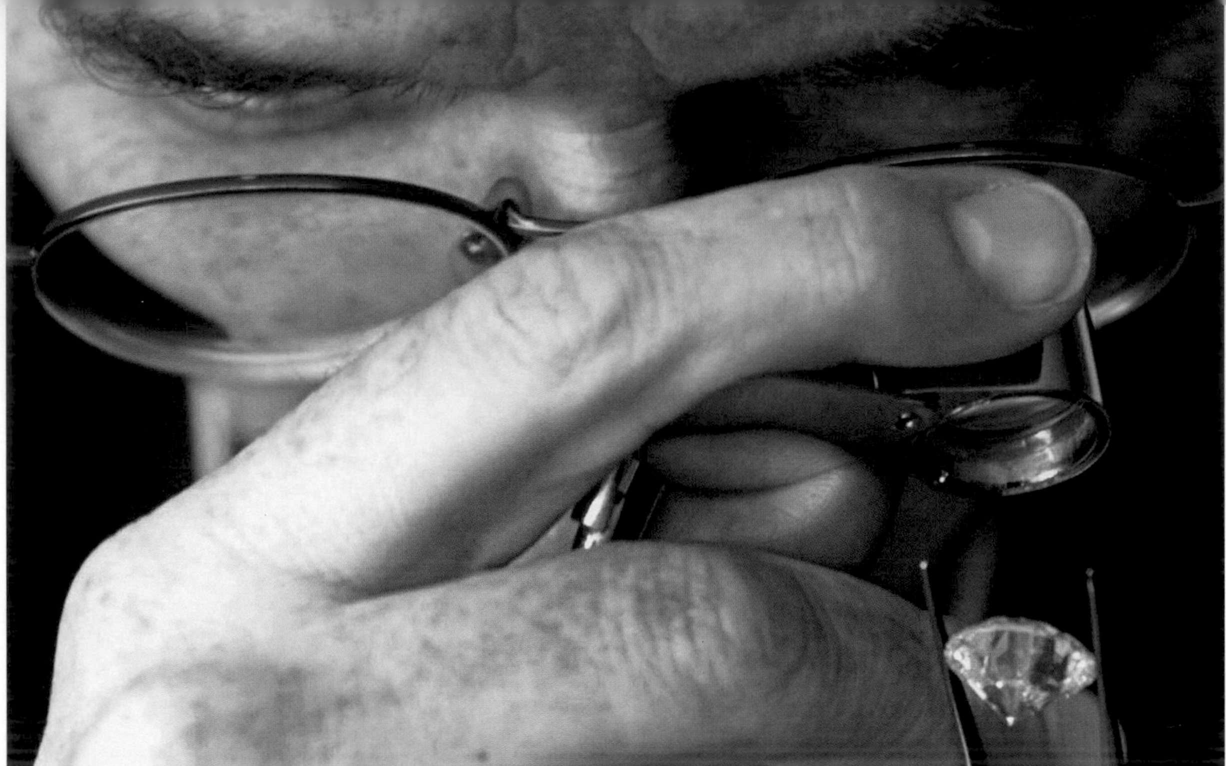

A merchant examines an eleven-karat diamond. Israel exported more than $6 billion worth of polished diamonds in 2004.

International Connections

The United States has been Israel's biggest trading partner since 1985. Israel also has a strong business connection with western Europe because they are geographically close. Japan and China exchange steel products, heavy equipment, fish, and other products for Israeli high-tech equipment, chemicals, and other industrial goods. Israel also exports cut diamonds, high-tech products, wood and paper products, and textiles.

Keeping in Touch

Israelis have plenty of ways of keeping in touch with each other and with the world. It seems that almost everyone in Israel has a cell phone, from the desert Bedouin to the corporate executive. Israel has one national television network geared to Israelis and another aimed outside the country to its

Arab neighbors. There are also five national radio networks and one short wave radio network for overseas. In 1993, cable TV was introduced to Israel. About 70 percent of the country was hooked up by 2002.

Israelis love to read. They delve into magazines covering entertainment, sports, fashion, the arts, and other subjects. Everyone rushes to get their daily newspapers, published in Hebrew, Russian, Arabic, Yiddish, English, Hungarian, French, German, or Polish. *Ma'ariv* ("Evening") and *Yediot Aharonot* ("Latest News") are the primary Hebrew-language daily newspapers. The principal Arabic-language daily is *Al Anba* ("The News"). The major English-language daily paper is the *Jerusalem Post*.

In 2002, 66 percent of Israelis owned a cell phone. The country has more cell phones than it has fixed phone lines.

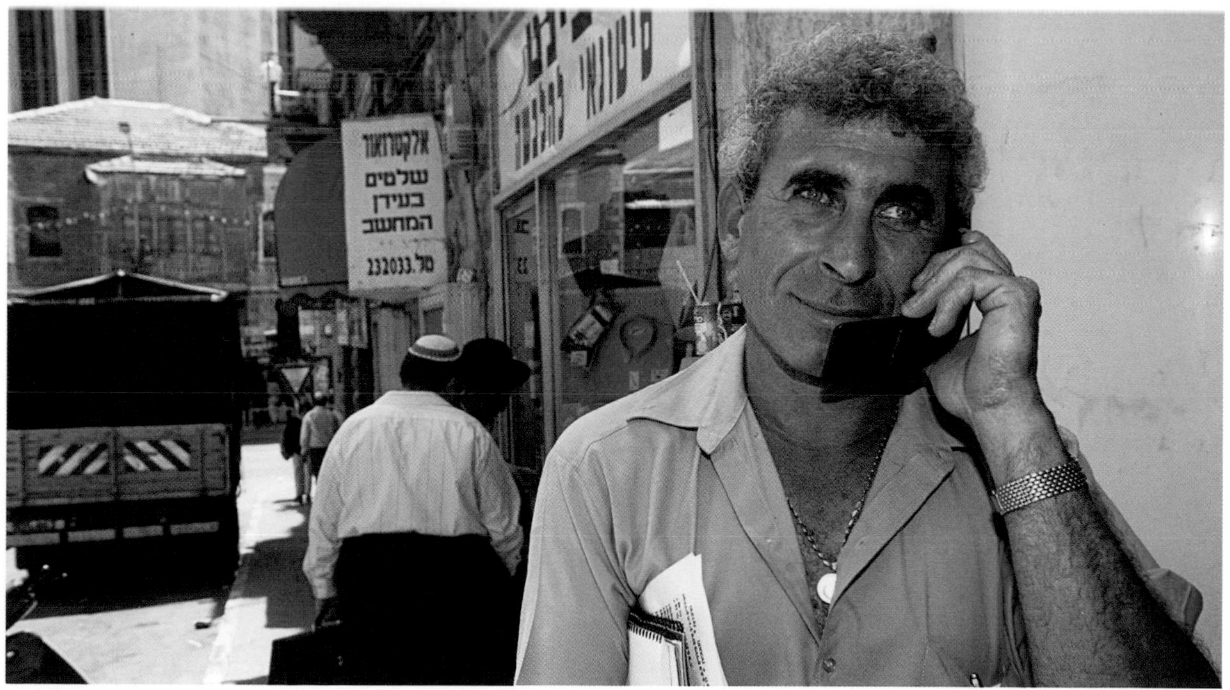

Transportation Systems

It is easy to get around Israel, with its 10,500 miles (16,898 km) of paved highways. Major rail lines, used mostly for freight, cover 400 miles (640 km), linking major cities and industrial areas. A rapid-transit urban rail system links Tel Aviv with its suburbs. Buses are the most popular form of public transportation.

Israel's national airline is El Al. Serving a mostly Jewish population, El Al conforms to Jewish law. Kosher food, which adheres to the dietary laws followed by many Jews, is served on El Al flights, and the airline does not fly on the Sabbath, from Friday evening to Saturday evening. When it is time to pray on El Al flights, Orthodox men gather for services at the front or rear of their plane, as they would in a synagogue.

A train passes through the Soreq Valley between Tel Aviv and Jerusalem. In Israel, train travel is less common than bus travel.

Getting Around

Sherut taxis are shared cabs, often the size of minivans, that operate on fixed routes within cities and to and from Ben-Gurion Airport in Tel Aviv. Regular cabs can be picked up outside hotels, bus and train stations, and at the airport. Urban buses operate regularly in the cities, but there is no bus service on the Sabbath.

To save money, many young people hitchhike in Israel. The practice is becoming less common, however, because of potential terrorist attacks. Despite the danger, groups of schoolchildren or soldiers loaded down with military gear can still be seen thumbing a ride.

Because of the threat of hijackings and violence, El Al places a high priority on security. Armed guards are stationed at all El Al ticket counters. Careful screening of passengers and luggage takes place before anyone gets on a plane. Undercover officers ride on the planes.

Haifa is Israel's main seaport. Other ports include Ashdod, Ashqelon, Eilat, Hadera, and Tel Aviv-Jaffa. Ferry services run to and from Greece, Cyprus, and Italy. Israel is easy to reach—for pleasure or for business.

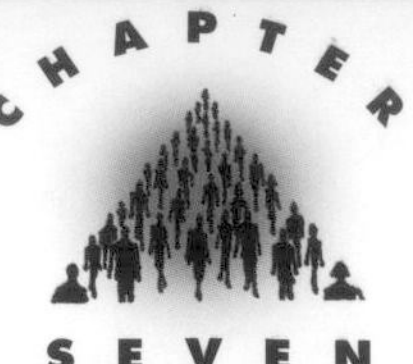

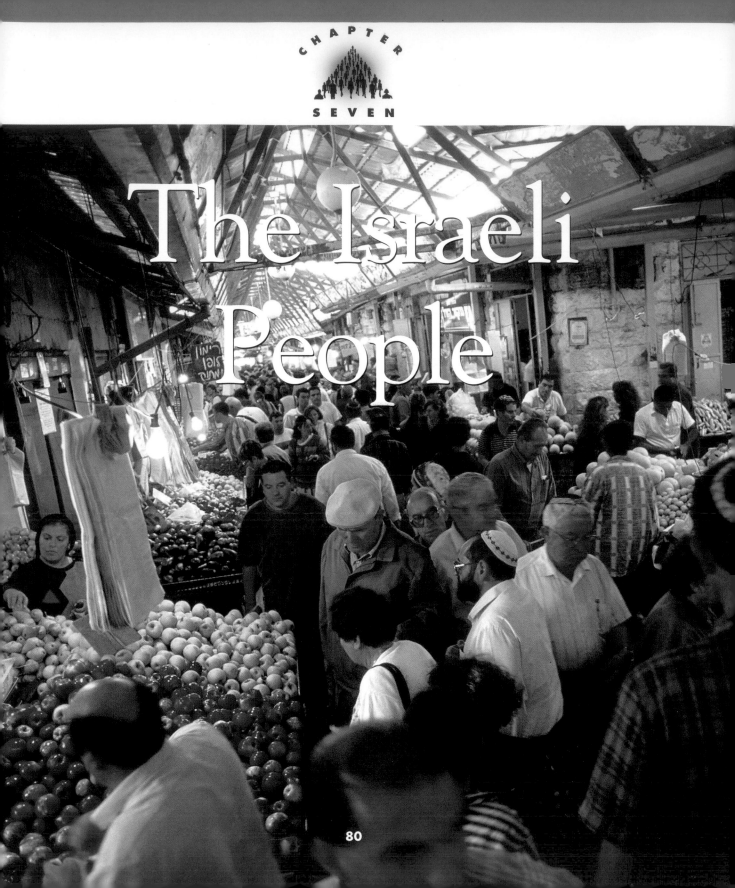

The Israeli People

Israel has more than six million citizens, 80 percent of whom are Jews. Muslims, Druze, and Christians make up most of the rest of the population. After Israel was founded in 1948, Jews from around the world emigrated to their new nation. They brought their skills, traditions, and cultures from the Far East, Africa, Europe, and the Americas. Israel is a melting pot of heritages.

Opposite: **People come to Mahanei Yehuda in Jerusalem to buy fruits and vegetables.**

A Rainbow People

Palestine was rough and mostly barren at the end of the 1800s, but settlers worked diligently to make the desert flower. Before 1948, most of the Jewish settlers in Palestine came from central and eastern Europe. Often they came to escape religious persecution, seeking safety in the Holy Land. After World War II, almost two million Jews came from North Africa and Arab lands such as Yemen. In the 1990s, hundreds of thousands of Russians made up another great wave of newcomers. In 1991, thousands of Ethiopian

Jewish immigrants stand at the railing of a ship as they arrive in Israel in 1948. Nearly seven hundred thousand Jews moved to Israel in its first four years of statehood.

Israel's Ethnic Breakdown

Jewish	80%
Non-Jewish (mostly Arab)	20%

Jews were airlifted to Israel in what was called Operation Solomon. Many highly educated Jews from Canada, the United States, South Africa, and other countries have also come to live in their spiritual homeland.

Israel is a young country, with 27 percent of the population under 15 years old. Another 63 percent are between 15 and 64. Only 10 percent are older than 65. Life expectancy in 2000 was 80.9 years for females and 76.7 years for males.

Native-Born "Sabras"

By the year 2000, more than 50 percent of Israelis had been born in the country. The Israeli natives are proud to call themselves *sabras*, literally "prickly pears." Prickly pears are a type of cactus that have fruit that is tough on the outside but sweet on the inside. These hardy plants can grow anywhere in

Arabs are the largest minority in Israel. They are mainly concentrated in the Galilee in northern Israel, in central Israel just west of the West Bank, and in the Negev.

the Middle East's harsh climate and poor soil. Just like the prickly pear, the Israelis have flourished.

Arab Israelis

Muslim Arabs are the second-largest ethnic group in Israel. Most belong to the Sunni sect of Islam. Arabs have their own schools within the Israeli school system. They also have their own political parties, businesses, and local administrators. Jaffa, an ancient Mediterranean seaport next to Tel Aviv, has a large number of Arab residents. In much of Jaffa, Jews and Arabs don't mix, but that is not always the case. After parties at Jaffa's hot nightspots, some Jewish, Muslim, and Christian young people gather at a bakery in the old city. There they can always get a snack before heading home. The shop is run by an Israeli Arab family long active in politics and community affairs. The crowded street outside the tiny shop shows the bright face of a new Israel, a face of many complexions, beliefs, and heritages.

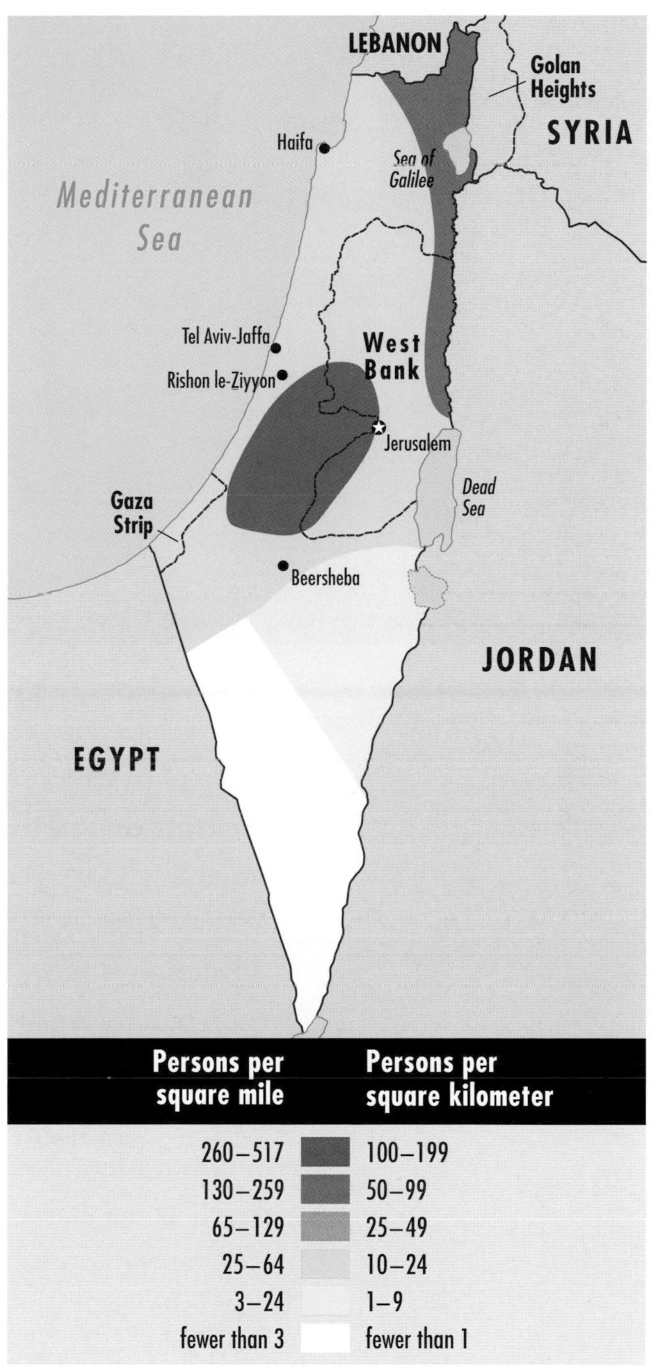

Girls at a religious school in Ashquelon. Israel is home to about 350,000 high school students.

The School System

Nearly two million young people attend school in Israel. They are enrolled in state schools, state religious schools, and independent schools. About 70 percent of Israeli children attend the state schools that are nonreligious.

Israel also has a separate Arab and Druze school system, which pupils may attend if their parents wish. Youngsters from ages five to sixteen must attend school. Primary education runs from grades one through six. Grades seven through nine are junior high school. Tenth through twelfth grades are high school. Israel has three types of high schools. General academic schools teach history, math, languages, social studies, geography, and economics. Students can also attend vocational high schools or agricultural high schools.

On to College

Students must pass a tough national exam in order to go to a university. There are a number of institutions of higher learning in Israel. Among them are Bar-Ilan University/Ramat Gan, Ben-Gurion University, Hebrew University of Jerusalem, Open University of Israel, Technion/Israel Institute of Technology, Tel Aviv University, University of Haifa, and Weizmann Institute of Science.

College campuses are packed with young and old Israelis and exchange students from other countries. Streets near the campuses are crowded with motorbikes and bicycles. Buses constantly load and unload book-carrying students. Nearby neighborhoods overflow with trendy coffee shops and well-stocked bookstores.

The Ben-Gurion University of the Negev in Beersheba was founded in 1967 in the Galilee region of North Israel. The school is well-known for its work in desert research and medicine.

Jewish Consciousness

In the 1950s and 1960s, a Jewish Consciousness program was put into place in the nonreligious schools. The program was intended to teach youngsters what it means to be Jewish. But the hard lessons learned during Israel's wars probably did more to emphasize Jewish consciousness than any textbook could ever do.

The Hall of Names at the Yad Vashem Holocaust Memorial Museum displays pictures of victims of the Holocaust. Six million Jews were slaughtered in Europe in the 1930s and 1940s.

Schoolchildren often take field trips to Jewish holy sites and to military museums where veterans tell their stories. Bringing one fateful chapter to life in their national story is Yad Vashem, the Museum of the Holocaust in Jerusalem. The complex provides a look at the horrors inflicted on the Jews

by the Nazis and their allies in Europe in the 1930s and 1940s.

Yad Vashem sits on a hilltop overlooking a quiet valley filled with memorials to destroyed villages. An underground chamber at the museum is dedicated to children who died in the Holocaust. The chamber is lit by a few candles, whose flames are reflected by mirrors, creating what looks like hundreds of tiny stars. In the background are heard the soft cries of children and a repeated whispered reading of hundreds of names of the dead. Trees are planted around the museum in memory of "the Righteous," non-Jews who helped Jews escape the Nazis. Nobody talks very loudly after emerging from Yad Vashem.

Living through the Holocaust

During World War II, the Nazis rounded up European Jews and put them in concentration camps. Millions of Jews were murdered in these camps. Fanny Ben-Aris wrote the following poem in a concentration camp when she was nine years old. It is on display at Yad Vashem.

It's night
All is calm
The birds
Still send
Some cries
To their comrades and
To the sun
Night has come
Like a curtain that is drawn
Slowly, slowly.
Night is born
Words on a black cloud
Here is the moon
And in the rooms
They sleep with glimpses
Of dreams in their eyes.

Official Languages

Hebrew and Arabic are the official languages of Israel. Hebrew was spoken by the ancient Israelites in the biblical era. Some of its sounds are formed toward the back of the throat, giving Hebrew a guttural sound. The language is similar to others spoken in the Middle East. It is believed that today's Hebrew has its roots with the Canaanites who inhabited Canaan (Palestine) centuries before the Israelites arrived. In fact,

Common Hebrew Words and Phrases

Shalom	Hello *or* Good-bye
Boker tov	Good morning
Erev tov	Good evening
Ken	Yes
Lo	No
Toda	Thank you
Bevakasha	Please *or* You're welcome

Common Arabic Words and Phrases

Salaam aleikum	Hello (formal)
Marhaba	Hello (informal)
Aleikum as-salaam	(response to "Hello")
Sabah al-kheir	Good morning
Masa' al-kheir	Good evening
Aiwa	Yes
La	No
Shukran	Thank you
Min fadlak	Please (to a man)
Min fadlik	Please (to a woman)

the Israelites called their language "the speech of Canaan." However, scholars now know that there were some slight differences between the Hebrew dialects spoken in the area. Most of the Old Testament of the Bible was written in Hebrew.

Over the centuries, the Jewish people were influenced by other people in the region, who spoke Aramaic. Hebrew became more of a "classical" language, used in religious services and by scholars, poets, and authors. Aramaic became the language of the ordinary people. Translating Hebrew manuscripts written long ago is difficult because words and meanings have changed over time.

Arabic, one of the principal tongues of the world, is the second most common language in Israel. It is used by Israeli Arabs both for prayer and for everyday life, and by workers who come into Israel from Jordan or other Arab regions. Jewish Israeli citizens of Arabic heritage also speak Arabic.

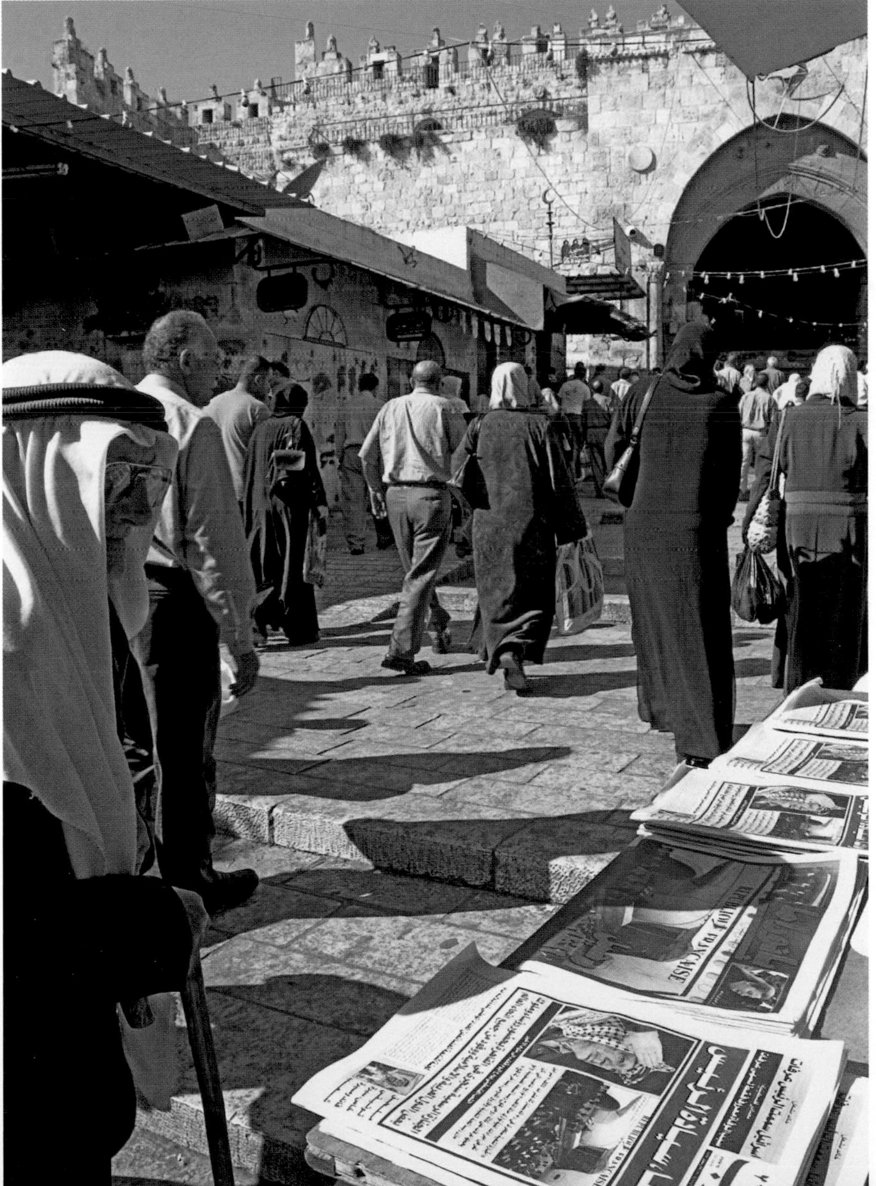

A man looks at an Arabic-language newspaper in Jerusalem. About 20 percent of Israelis speak Arabic.

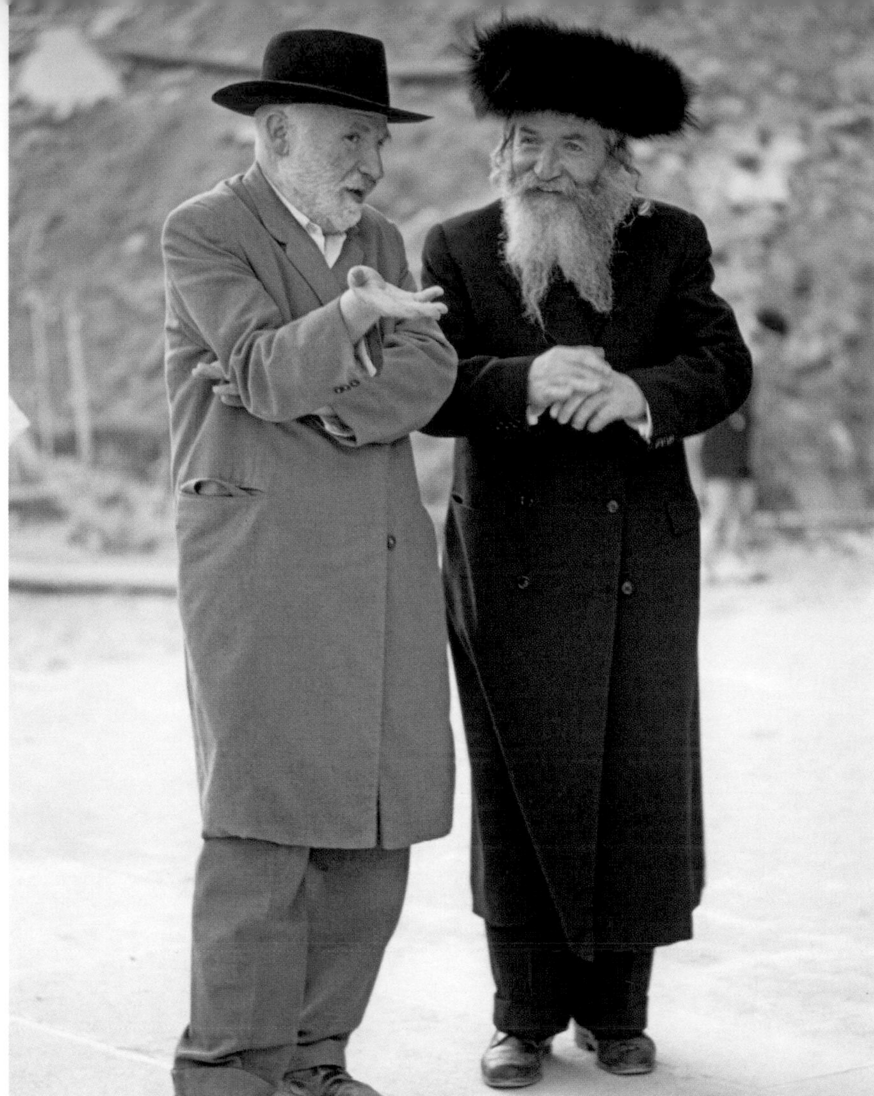

Millions of Jews from all over the world immigrated to Israel in the twentieth century, bringing their languages with them. Many Jews from Europe speak Yiddish.

Other Languages

Some older Israelis still speak Yiddish, a language once used by many European Jews. A mixture of German, Slavic languages, and Hebrew, Yiddish originated in the twelfth century in Germany. Every country in which the Jews lived also contributed words and pronunciations, but a French Jew speaking Yiddish can generally understand a Polish or Italian Jew speaking Yiddish.

Because Israel is a nation of immigrants, many other languages are also spoken in the country. So many Russians moved to Israel in the early 1990s that people began to joke that Hebrew was Israel's second language, implying that more people spoke Russian. Other Israelis speak Italian, Polish, Spanish, or various African languages. Almost everyone can speak English, which is a required subject in state schools.

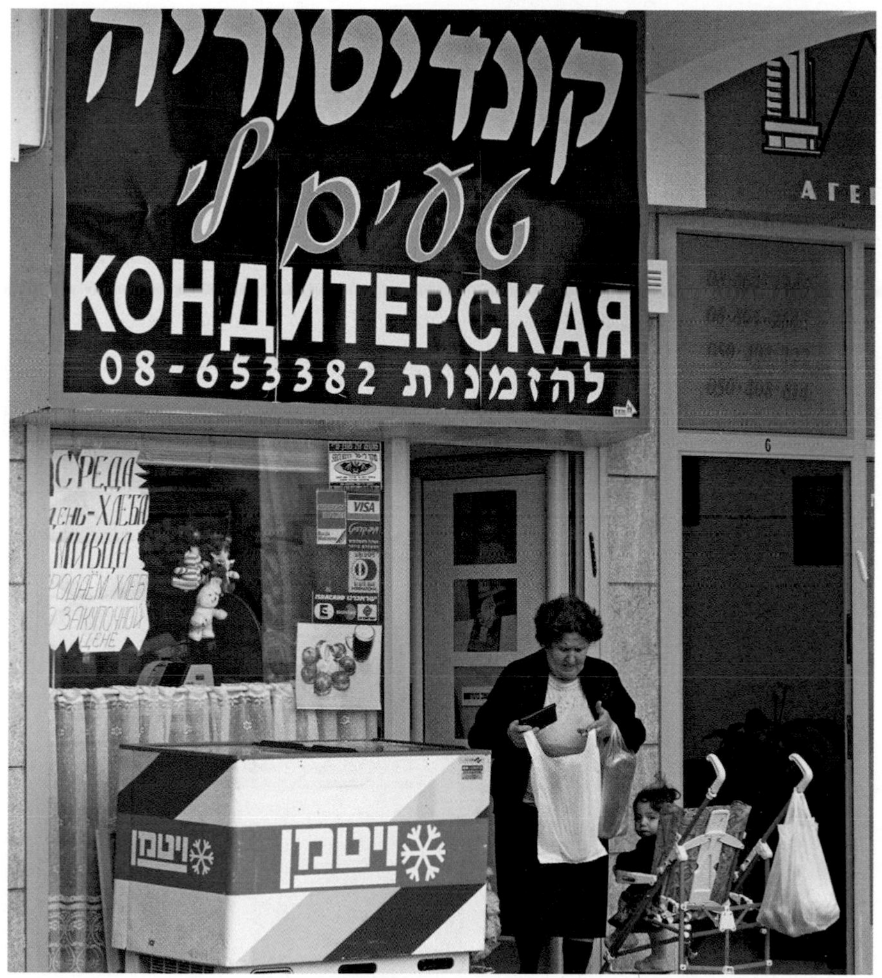

Nearly a million Russians live in Israel, so many shops have signs in both Russian and Hebrew.

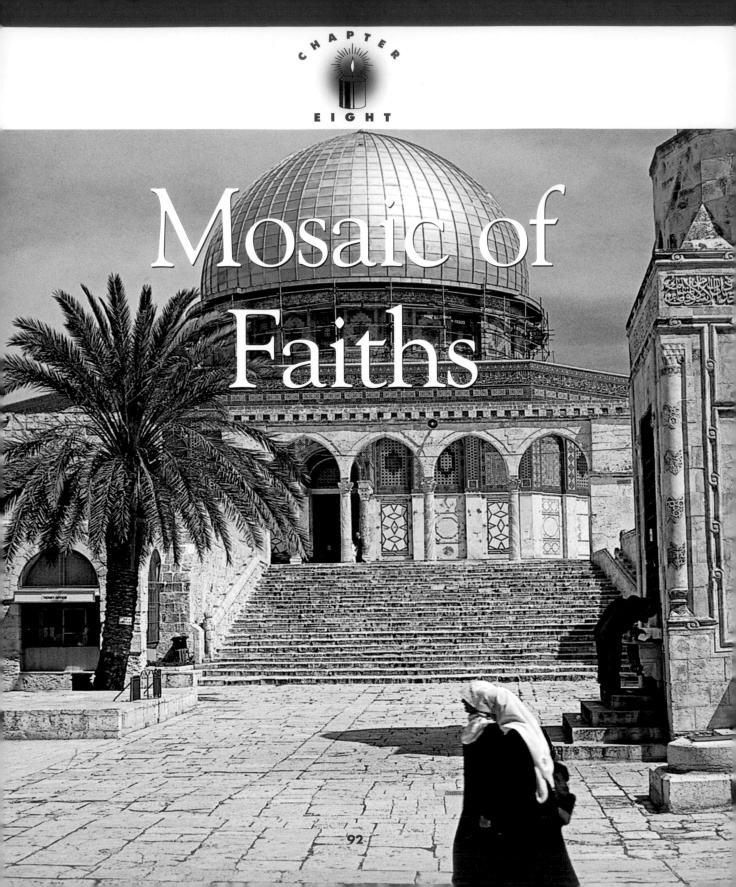

Mosaic of Faiths

Nothing regarding religion in the Middle East is simple. Any expression of religion can become a political statement. Before Israel became an independent nation, many countries jockeyed for power in Palestine. They used religion to gain a foothold for their own ambitions. As an example, Russia had authority over Greek and Russian Orthodox shrine sites. France protected the monasteries of the Roman Catholic Church. Britain and Prussia (a country that later

Opposite: **The Dome of the Rock in Jerusalem is one of the world's most famous Muslim shrines.**

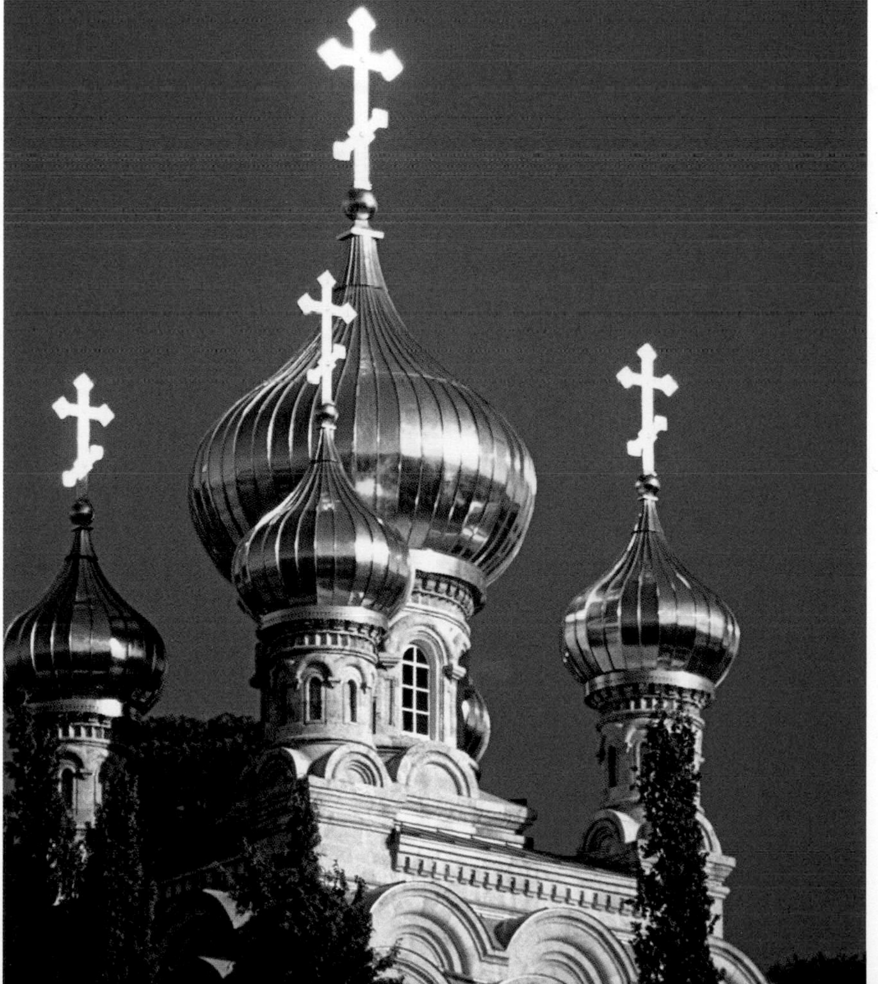

The Saint Mary Magdalene Russian Orthodox church in Jerusalem sports seven gold onion-shaped domes.

became part of Germany) kept watch over the few Protestant churches. Britain eventually extended its security umbrella over the Jews.

Judaism

Judaism is the oldest of the world's major religions and the first that expressed a belief in only one god. Jewish beliefs are laid out in the Hebrew Bible, which is the Old Testament of the Christian Bible. Judaism's most basic teachings are found in the Torah, the first five books of the Hebrew Bible. Judaism places a strong emphasis on ethical teaching and study.

The synagogue is the Jewish house of worship. In Judaism, the spiritual leader is called a rabbi. Members of each synagogue choose their own rabbi.

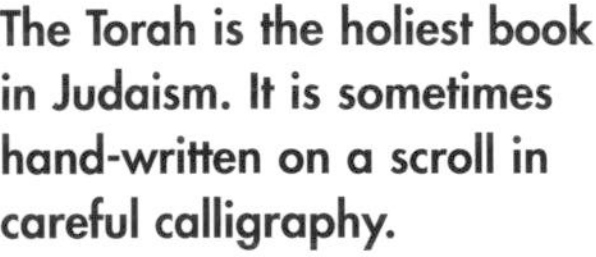

The Torah is the holiest book in Judaism. It is sometimes hand-written on a scroll in careful calligraphy.

Judaism has broken into different branches. Orthodox Jews follow the old traditions. They strictly observe Jewish laws such as praying three times a day and doing no work on the Sabbath. About 20 percent of Israeli Jews are Orthodox. Conservative and Reform Jews have been more willing to blend in with the modern world. Conservative Jews follow many of the traditional laws. Many Reform Jews, on the other hand, find moral teachings more important than following traditional laws.

Religions of Israel

Judaism	77%
Islam	16%
Christianity	2%
Druze	2%
Unspecified	4%

Does not equal 100% due to rounding

Religious Challenges

Since independence, Israelis have wrestled with challenges. They needed to merge a secular state with the religious traditions of a people whose survival over the centuries had depended on protecting their spiritual way of life. Controversy is nothing new. Not only do representatives of the different religions in Israel often argue, but the Jewish religious minority and nonreligious majority are often at odds. Religious political parties often hold the balance of power in the Israeli government.

In addition, the question, Who is a Jew? is important. Today, under the country's Law of Return, a Jew automatically becomes a citizen when making an *aliyah* (immigration to Israel). But some Orthodox Jews want to limit the definition of who actually qualifies. They believe that the only people who should be granted automatic citizenship are those born of Jewish mothers or those who converted to the faith according to traditional Jewish law, or *halacha*.

Some Orthodox Jewish groups even refuse to recognize the State of Israel. They argue that a nation of God cannot be forced to obey secular law. Israel's need to deal fairly with its Muslim and Christian citizens also causes disagreements. Resolving such issues remains a difficult task for Israelis, no matter their religion.

Clothing Is Political

Some Jewish men wear yarmulkes all day. Others wear them only during prayer.

Articles of clothing hint at a Jew's political and religious persuasion. A yarmulke is a small cap worn by Orthodox, Conservative, and many Reform Jews during prayer. Some men wear yarmulkes at all times, even though the religious laws do not require it. Conservative Jews tend to wear black yarmulkes, while more liberal Jews often wear light-colored or white crocheted yarmulkes. Even in the media, references are often made to disputes between the "Black Hats" and the "Crocheted Caps" because it is an easy way to identify the factions.

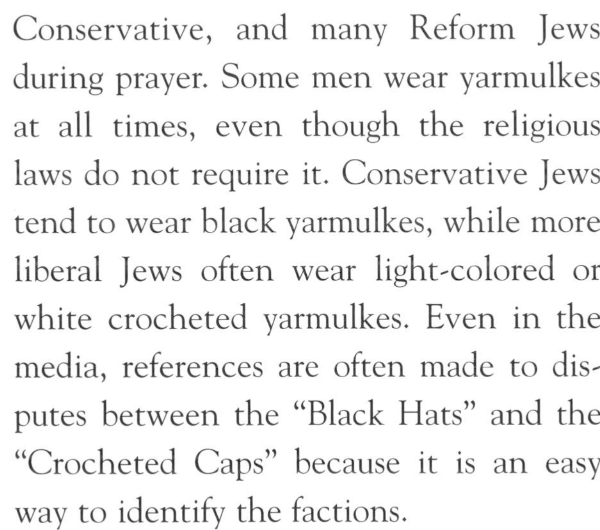

When praying, reverent Jewish men wear a *tallith*, a fringed, four-cornered shawl. They then strap *tefillin*, black boxes containing writings from the Torah (Jewish law), to their hands and foreheads. This fulfills a biblical instruction that says, "You shall bind them as a sign on your hand and as frontlets between your eyes."

Haredim men gather for a funeral in Jerusalem. The haredi make up about a third of Jerusalem's population.

Strict Orthodox communities are called *haredi* ("God-fearing"), and their members are called *haredim*. Depending on their sect, Orthodox men wear a black coat; long sidelocks (sideburns that are long and curled); and a black, broad-brimmed hat that is sometimes trimmed with fur. This shows that they are separate from the world. Orthodox women always keep their heads covered and dress modestly with both arms and legs covered.

Jerusalem's Mea Shearim is one haredi neighborhood. Central to its lifestyle are the religious schools, called yeshivas. There students study the Torah and read the Talmud, a collection of Jewish laws and their interpretations. From the age of four until marriage, and often long afterward, male heredim spend most of their day poring over these verses. A yeshiva is not a quiet place. Arguments over the meaning and interpretations of the Scriptures are part of the learning process. The students loudly repeat the lessons chanted by their

Pilgrims at the Wailing Wall

The holiest place for Jews in Israel is the remains of the Western Wall of the Second Temple in Jerusalem. Most of this temple was destroyed by the Romans in A.D. 70. The Western Wall was held by Jordan from 1948 until 1967, when Israeli paratroopers gained control of it in the Six-Day War. Soldiers swear an oath of allegiance to Israel during ceremonies there, with rifles and machine guns lined up alongside prayer books.

Sometimes called the "Wailing Wall," the Western Wall attracts tens of thousands of pilgrims every year. The pilgrims chant the *kinot* (dirges) and lament the fall of Jerusalem and loss of the temple. A *mechitsah,* a barricade in the wide courtyard in front of the wall, separates praying Orthodox men from women. The wall is a popular spot for *bar mitzvahs* and *bat mitzvahs,* Jewish ceremonies signifying the passage of boys and girls into adulthood. All guests must cover their heads when they visit the Wailing Wall.

teachers. Some yeshiva students are exempt from serving in the military, while others continue their studies while serving in the military.

In the early 2000s, there were about fifty thousand yeshiva students. The number is growing because of the high birthrate in haredi families. Ten or more children is not uncommon because haredim take to heart the biblical passage "be fruitful and multiply."

Festivals and the Sabbath

The Jewish Sabbath and religious festivals are strictly observed in Israel. Most shops, factories, farms, offices, and restaurants close from sunset Friday to sunset Saturday. Even public transportation halts. But taxis still operate, and private cars crowd the roads. Soccer matches are played, and crowds head to the beach or to a park for a picnic. This irritates some of the more Orthodox Jews, who think the day should be reserved for religious activities.

Prior to Yom Kippur, some Jews take part in a ceremony called *kaporot* in which a chicken is swung over the head. This is supposed to transfer the person's sin to the chicken, which is then killed and given to the poor.

"*Leshanah tovah tikatevu,*" ("May you be inscribed for a happy new year") is a blessing heard in every Jewish home around the world on Rosh Hashanah, the Jewish New Year. Other celebrations include Yom Kippur (the Day of Atonement) and Purim, which recalls the biblical figure Esther's deliverance of her people from a massacre by Haman, a courtier of her husband, King Ahasuerus. Passover marks the exodus of the Jewish slaves from Egypt. An end-of-harvest festival is called the feast of Sukkot.

An ancient Qur'an in Jerusalem. The Qur'an was written in an early form of classical Arabic.

Following the Qur'an

The word *Islam* means "submission to God" in Arabic. Followers of Islam, called Muslims, make up about 15 percent of the Israeli population. Muslims follow the teachings outlined in the Qur'an, which is their guide to everything in life. Muslims believe the Qur'an's contents were revealed to the prophet Muhammad by God, or *Allah* in Arabic.

Muhammad lived in the Arabian town of Mecca. He objected to the paganism of people around him, but few people listened to him. He and his followers were chased away into the desert in A.D. 622.

Muhammad organized an army and soon defeated his enemies. Muslim forces eventually swept through the entire Middle East, much of Africa, and into southern Europe and Asia. Before a battle, they would shout, "There is no god but Allah and Muhammad is His prophet." Muslims around the world today proclaim this belief daily.

As Muslims gained control of the Middle East, they took over many Christian holy sites. But some Christians wanted to reclaim these shrines and drive the Muslims out of the Holy Land. Beginning in 1096, Christians from Europe launched eight major Crusades, or military expeditions, into the Holy Land. They were only partly successful battling great Muslim

Over 1.6 million worshippers attend the annual pilgrimage rituals in Mecca, Saudi Arabia. Pilgrims pray at the Grand Mosque.

leaders such as Salāh ad-Dīn (Saladin). Ruins of Crusader castles still dot the Israeli landscape.

Old Traditions

Muslims follow centuries-old traditions. The faithful pray five times daily, facing in the direction of Mecca. Traditionally, a crier stood on a balcony high atop a minaret (a tower attached to a mosque) to call the faithful to prayer. Today, a recording is often played from the minaret instead. Other duties of Muslims include giving help to the poor and fasting (eating little or nothing) during Ramadan, the ninth month of the Muslim year. During Ramadam, Muslims fast between sunrise and sunset. A big feast marks the welcome end of the fast. At least once in their lives, devout Muslims who can afford it must also make a pilgrimage to the holy city of Mecca.

The Dome of the Rock

Jerusalem's Dome of the Rock, one of the holiest shrines in Islam, is easy to identify. Much photographed, this ancient building glows in the sun. In 1994, Jordan's King Hussein donated 176 pounds (80 kilograms) of gold to recoat the surface of the dome. The building was constructed in the seventh century to enclose a shrine to Muhammad. It is said that on this site the prophet Abraham offered his son Isaac for sacrifice. This is also the rock from which Muhammad is believed to have ascended to heaven.

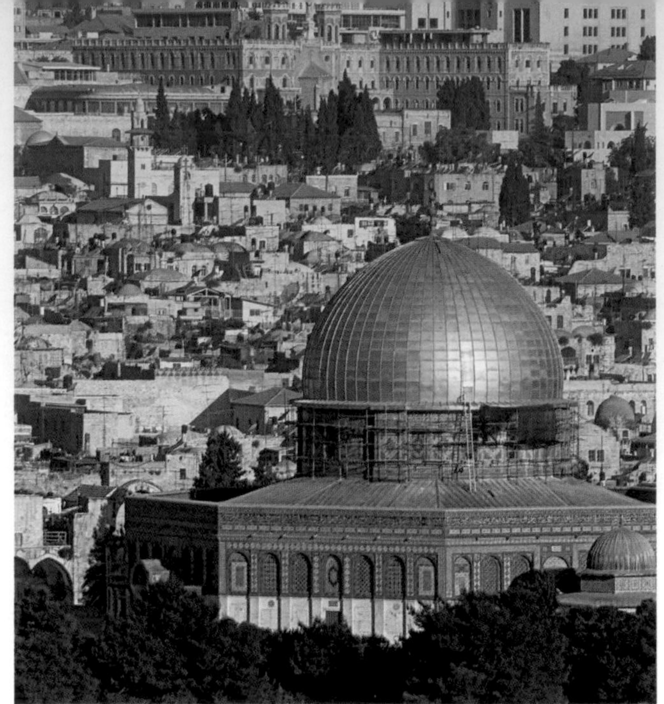

Friday is the Muslim holy day, when Muslims do not work. In Israel, Muslim holy days and festivals are officially recognized by the state. The Arabic station on the Israel Broadcasting Authority airs daily readings from the Qur'an, as well as sermons on Fridays.

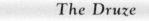

The Druze

The Israeli Druze are Arabic speakers who follow a secretive religion that broke from Islam almost a thousand years ago. The Druze name is derived from that of al-Darazi, one of the religion's founders. The Druze believe that souls pass from one body to another after death. They also believe Caliph al-Hakim bi'Amr Allah was god. He mysteriously disappeared in 1021 in Egypt. To become a Druze, a person must be born into the community—no converts have been accepted by the Druze since 1034.

The Druze have few ceremonies or rituals, but they do make pilgrimages to the grave of Jetro, Moses' father-in-law, which is near Karnei-Hittim in Galilee. The Druze, who are known for their hospitality, have easily blended in with the rest of Israeli society. They share their homes and food with visitors. They are also noted for their fighting abilities, and many Druze have become officers in the army and border patrol.

Druze elders gather to honor a soldier's bravery. About 106,000 Druze live in Israel.

A Holy Tomb

The Baha'i faith is named after its founder, Bahá'u'lláh ("the splendor of God"). Members of the Baha'i faith consider his tomb near Acre the holiest place on earth. Baha'i developed out of a Muslim mystical movement that arose in the 1840s. Promoting unity among all people and equal rights for men and women are among Baha'i tenets, or laws. The Baha'i were glad to see Zionist Jews moving back to Israel at the end of the nineteenth century. They believed that this had been foretold in the writings of their spiritual leaders. The Baha'i were among the first non-Jews to recognize the new State of Israel.

Christians in the Holy Land

Almost every large branch of Christianity is represented in Israel. The most ancient Christian group is the Greek Orthodox, established in the Holy Land as early as the second century after Jesus's death. It remains the only Christian religious community headquartered in Israel today.

Israel is home to Russian, Syrian, Armenian, and Ethiopian Orthodox churches. Dozens of Roman Catholic religious groups are represented in Israel—including thirty communities of nuns, each with their own convent. The Uniates, a sect

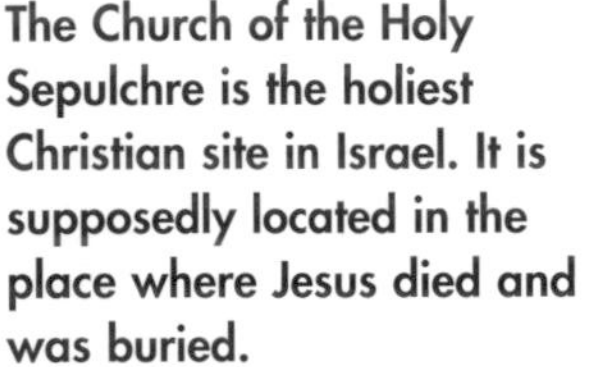

The Church of the Holy Sepulchre is the holiest Christian site in Israel. It is supposedly located in the place where Jesus died and was buried.

linked with the Roman Catholic Church, live mainly along the border with Lebanon. Israel is also home to Episcopalians, Lutherans, and other Protestant Christians.

Small Communities

Several smaller religious communities also thrive in Israel. These include a group of Black Hebrews, a non-Jewish religious group whose members come from Atlanta, Chicago, Washington, and other U.S. cities. Although they are not Israeli citizens, the government settled them in the Negev city of Dimona. They maintain their own schools and social institutions.

Black Hebrews first came to Israel in 1969. They claim to be descended from Jews who were forced from Jerusalem in A.D. 70.

The Karaites recognize the Scripture as the only direct source of religious law. Over the centuries, they evolved from a mix of traditions including Judaism and Arab and other Middle Eastern cultures.

The Samaritans are an independent people who trace their origins far back into the Scripture. They lived in the Holy Land at least two thousand years before the birth of Jesus. They believe that Moses is the sole prophet of God. Samaritans also expect that a "restorer" will return on the Last Day of Earth and lead his chosen people, including the Samaritans, to paradise.

Arts and Sports

Regardless of their religious or ethnic backgrounds, most Israelis take arts and sports seriously. Israeli performing artists are world renowned. The natural beauty of Israel provides a landscape perfect for renditions by painters and photographers whose creativity takes many forms. On the athletic side, Israelis avidly follow their favorite basketball team, and kids eagerly seek autographs of the top soccer players. Many Israelis belong to amateur sports leagues. Easy access to the ocean, the desert, and mountains provides a wide variety of outdoor opportunities for many sports, from water skiing to hiking to rock climbing.

Opposite: ***Spring Path*** **by Ron Gang depicts the descent to Habesor Ravine.**

Israel's weather is perfect for enjoying outdoor activities. This water park is used throughout the year.

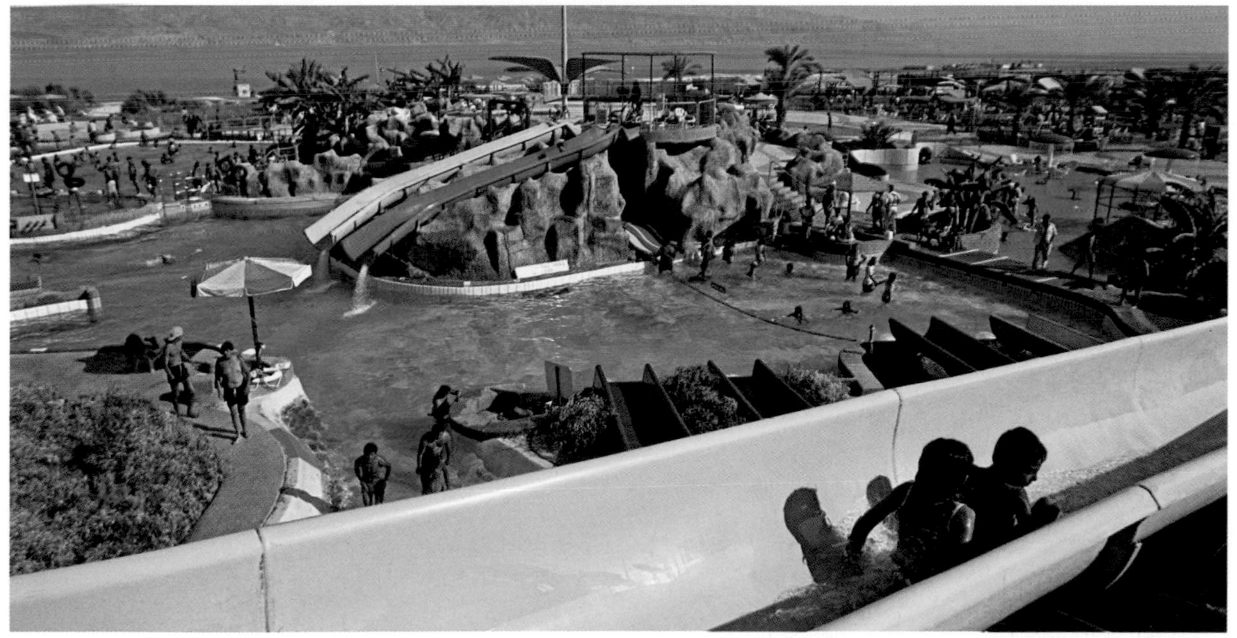

Writers

Many Israeli writers are unknown outside Israel, partly because Hebrew is not widely spoken elsewhere in the world. Shmuel Yosef Agnon (1888–1970) is the only Israeli to have won a Nobel Prize for Literature, the world's most prestigious writing award. Agnon grew up in Germany and often wrote in German. He moved to Israel in 1913. Agnon wrote novels and short stories about Jewish life that combine satire with religious themes. Among his best-known works are *A Simple Story* (1935), *The Bridal Canopy* (1937), and *Only Yesterday* (1945).

A National Poet

Hayim Nahman Bialik (1873–1934) is considered Israel's national poet. Born in the Ukraine, part of the old Soviet Union, Bialik worked for a publisher in Germany before coming to Palestine in 1924. Bialik, who wrote in Hebrew, was particularly famous for his works expressing Jewish identity and unity. His spacious Tel Aviv home, called *Beit Bialik* ("House of Bialik") was the unofficial center of the Writers' Association, the Committee of the Hebrew Language, and other arts groups. The house was opened to the public when he died and is now used for classes and lectures. Bialik's private library is available for use by visiting scholars. Tours go through the building daily, and almost every Israeli citizen has visited the house at some time or another, usually as a youngster during a school field trip.

But the word is getting out about the high quality of Israel's literary scene. Yehuda Amichai has composed eleven volumes of poetry since 1956, all of which have been translated from Hebrew into many languages, including Chinese and Japanese. In his poem "National Thoughts," Amichai writes about how his native language "was torn from its sleep in the Bible" to become a contemporary language.

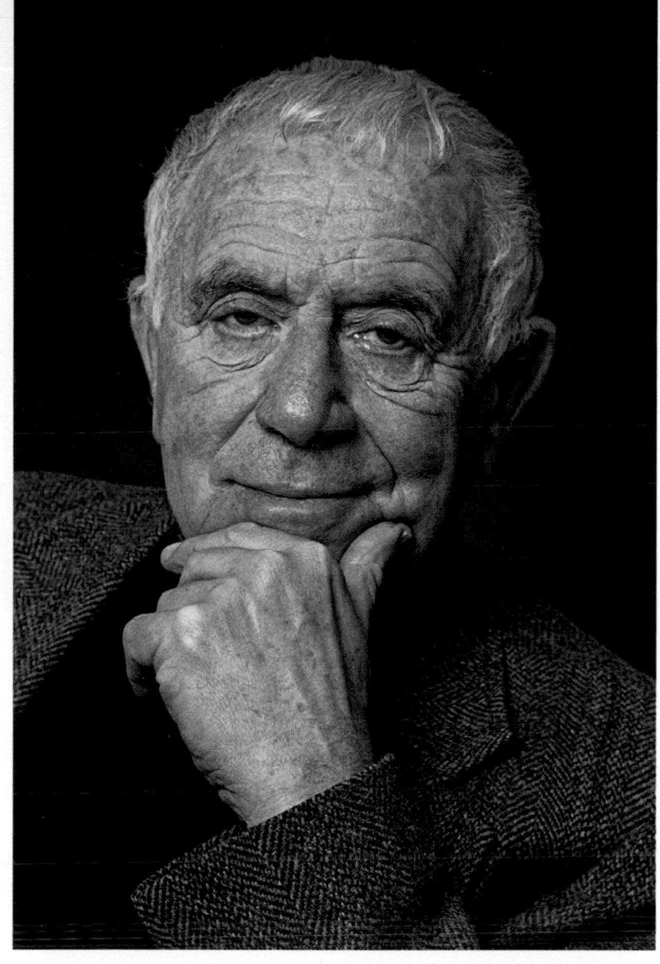

Born in Germany, Yehuda Amichai came to Israel with his family after the Nazis came to power. His poetry has been translated into thirty languages.

Zbigniew Herbert from Poland, Vasko Popa from the former Yugoslavia, Andrei Voznesensky from the former Soviet Union, and Robert Friend from the United States are other writers now proud to be Israelis. They write in Hebrew as well as in their native tongues. Phillip Hyams and Moshe Benarroch are typical of the new breed of Israeli literary figures who came from abroad. Poet-filmmaker Hyams was born in 1954 in Montreal, Canada, and Benarroch was born in 1959 in Tétouan, Morocco. Benarroch's book of poems entitled *Litany of the Immigrant* has heartfelt interpretations of a newcomer's feelings about Israel. Among the talented Israeli-born writers are Salman Masalha, born in 1953 in the Druze town of M'gar in central Galilee, and Sharon Ahsse, born in Ramat Gan in 1966.

Itzhak Perlman was born in Yaffa. He is considered one of the world's greatest violinists.

Music

Music has always been important to Israelis. The Israel Philharmonic Orchestra is internationally known for its sweeping sound. Noted guest musicians such as violinist Itzhak Perlman and pianist/conductor Daniel Barenboim, both Israelis, regularly appear at its concerts. The orchestra plays in the three-thousand-seat Mann Auditorium in Tel Aviv, the country's largest performance hall. The orchestra also regularly presents outdoor concerts in the Yarkon Park in Tel Aviv.

Jazz is popular in Israel as well. The Red Sea Jazz Festival is held each year in Eilat. Many young Israelis listen to rock and roll. They go to concerts by visiting stars from around the world, and they also like the sounds of local heroes such as the punk group Useless ID and activist musician Aviv Geffen. *Va'adat Kishut* ("Decoration Committee") is an all-female rock band that is hot on the scene. Nightclubs in Tel Aviv and Haifa stay open until the early hours of the morning. Music by groups such as Gemini Cricket, Wow Mom, D.J. Adi Lev, and Lipstik Sing keeps everyone dancing. Flashing strobe lights blast the interior of the clubs with brilliant explosions of red, green, and white. Smoke from dry ice fills the rooms, almost hiding the bands onstage. The loud, throbbing beat guarantees that no one will sit still for long.

Traditional music is also popular in Israel. Klezmer instrumental music started in eastern Europe during the seventeenth century. Its distinctive mix of drums, violins, and clarinets along with keyboard and tambourines is played at weddings and other celebrations. Clarinetist David Perkins is often called Israel's "Klezmer King" because of his creative modernizing of this musical style.

The Red Sea Jazz Festival began in 1987. Each August it draws tens of thousands of music fans to the city of Eilat.

A Rising Star of Dance

Ido Tadmor, one of the younger stars of contemporary Israeli dance, was born in Jerusalem in 1964. Tadmor danced for several of the country's major troupes before being invited to join the Lar Lubovitch Dance Company of New York in 1990. He founded his own company in 1995. Tadmor has performed all across Europe and at the prestigious Tokyo Festival for Contemporary Dance.

Dance

Israeli dancers are internationally known for their form, creativity, and style. The Israel Ballet Company is well received wherever it appears. Inbal, Batsheeva, and Bat Dor are the most popular modern dance troupes. Choreographers and producers such as Ohad Nahrin are known everywhere. In addition to the large troupes, smaller companies are continually forming, dancing, merging, and fading as young performers move from production to production.

The Suzanne Dellal Center for Dance and Theater hosts a wide variety of modern dance productions as well as concerts and plays. It has four performance halls and outdoor performance spaces.

Several kibbutzim have dance companies that give young dancers their first performance opportunities. Uri Ivgi was raised on Kibbutz Hulata and began dancing there in 1990. In 1994, he was awarded first prize as best dancer at the Suzanne Dellal International Dance Competition in Tel Aviv. The Suzanne Dellal Centre for Dance and Theatre is

Folk dancing is popular in Israel. Here, children perform at Teddy Maiha Stadium in Jerusalem.

hidden away in a corner of Neve Tzedek, one of Tel Aviv's oldest neighborhoods. Every day, eager students flock to see their country's top performers practice.

A well-known folk dance is the *hora*. This exuberant dance is enjoyed by all Israelis, regardless of their age.

Theater Classics

Amalia Eyal, spokesperson for the Haifa Municipal Theater, says Israel is the "paradise of theater." Venues such as the Arab Theater are constantly packed. Noted performers like Shimon Israeli are always in demand. Classic dramas such as Isaac Bashevis Singer's *Teibele and Her Demon* are often staged. Other plays touch on the Palestine-Israel conflict, the peace talks, and similar contemporary issues facing Israelis. Most plays are produced in Hebrew, but there are now Russian theater companies and groups representing other nationalities. Many playhouses offer English translation through headsets.

Asim Abu-Shakra

Asim Abu-Shakra (1961–1990) was a young Arab Israeli painter whose work was widely exhibited around the country. One of his main subjects was the cactus, which he drew in many shapes and positions. His paintings evoked his feelings as a Muslim living in a primarily Jewish community. In his short career, Abu-Shakra is credited with raising his country's consciousness about the position of the Arab in Israeli society.

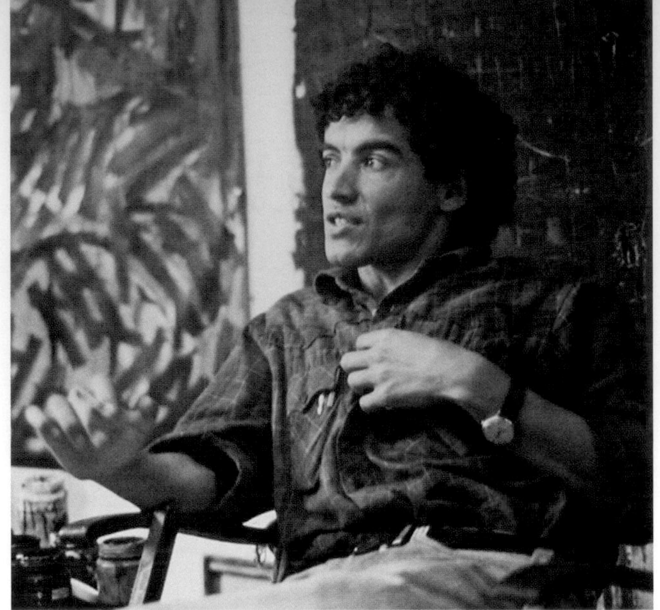

Israeli films are popular around the world. *Bonjour Monsieur Shlomi*, about a young boy taking care of his mixed-up family, was directed by Shemi Zarhin. The comedy won Best Film and Direction at the Moscow International Film Festival for Young People and was a highlight of the 2004 Israel Film Festival, which toured the United States.

Painting and Sculpture

The Museum of Contemporary Art in Tel Aviv and the Israel Museum in Jerusalem have some of the most extensive art collections in the world. Jewish benefactors from many countries have donated their personal collections, as well as money, to fill the country's largest museums. There are also many private galleries, such as the Ilana Goor Museum and Gallery, which stands in a narrow alley in the ancient seaport of Jaffa.

Zelig Segal proudly shows his intricate metalwork in a shop in Jerusalem's Designer Quarter, near the Old City's Jaffa Gate.

Designer Sam Phillipe displays his statues in major hotels. Both specialize in Judaica, artistic renditions of items of worship or pieces with Jewish themes. An entire colony of artists lives at Ein Hod, a colorful village south of Haifa. The Mediterranean Sea's soft breeze brushes the wind chimes hanging from porches and rustles colorful pennants draped from tree branches. Raya Zommer manages the village's Janco Dada Museum. A whimsical display by one of her artists featured live chickens! Another showcased "clothing" made of wire mesh.

The Tel Aviv Museum of Art features art from the sixteenth century to the present. The history of Palestine and the State of Israel are reflected in the Israeli Art Collection.

Sports

Israelis love sports of all kinds. They bowl, swim, parasail, climb mountains, ride horses, fish, race motorcycles and kayaks, shoot pool, and play card games. Rugby clubs such as ASA Tel Aviv and Rishon Lezion XV regularly battle for national championships.

The most popular team sports in Israel are soccer and basketball. Israel's national soccer team is one of the strongest in the Middle East. Fans love to cheer Coach Avraham Grant's players, especially defender Omri Afek, midfielder Haim Revivo, and all-around star Eyal Berkovic.

The powerhouse of the Israeli Basketball League is Maccabi Tel Aviv, a team that has won thirty-eight national titles since World War II. It captured twenty-three consecutive championships from 1970 to 1992. Maccabi also won the European basketball championships in 1977 and 1980. The most important game for Maccabi was its upset of CSKA Moscow, the Soviet Army team, during the 1977 tournament. The Israelis defeated the Soviets, 97–79. The game's Israeli hero was Tal Brody, a former all-American from the University of Illinois.

The Israeli national soccer team before a match in Dublin, Ireland. Soccer is one of the most popular sports in Israel.

The World Maccabiah Games

The World Maccabiah Games are the Jewish Olympics. They started in 1932 and have been held every four years since then, except during World War II. Events include swimming, wrestling, rowing, squash, bowling, track and field, softball, gymnastics, and other sports. Jewish athletes come to Israel from around the world to participate. Among the best ever was swimmer Mark Spitz of the United States, who won five gold medals at the 1972 Olympics.

Ice-skating and hockey have become popular in Israel. Ran Oz, who was born in Tel Aviv in 1977, is Israel's first native-born hockey star. Oz started to skate at age thirteen and quickly learned the game. In 1992, when he was only fourteen, Oz played in his first international tournament and went to Canada to continue his training. After military service, he became a championship defense player in the European League.

Israeli sailor Gal Fridman won a gold medal in windsurfing at the 2004 Olympics in Athens, Greece. It was the first time an Israeli had ever taken home Olympic gold. Fridman dedicated his medal to the memory of the eleven Israeli athletes and coaches killed by terrorists at the 1972 Olympics in Munich, Germany. Another Israeli, Arik Ze'evi, captured a bronze medal in Athens in judo.

Hurray for the Cousins

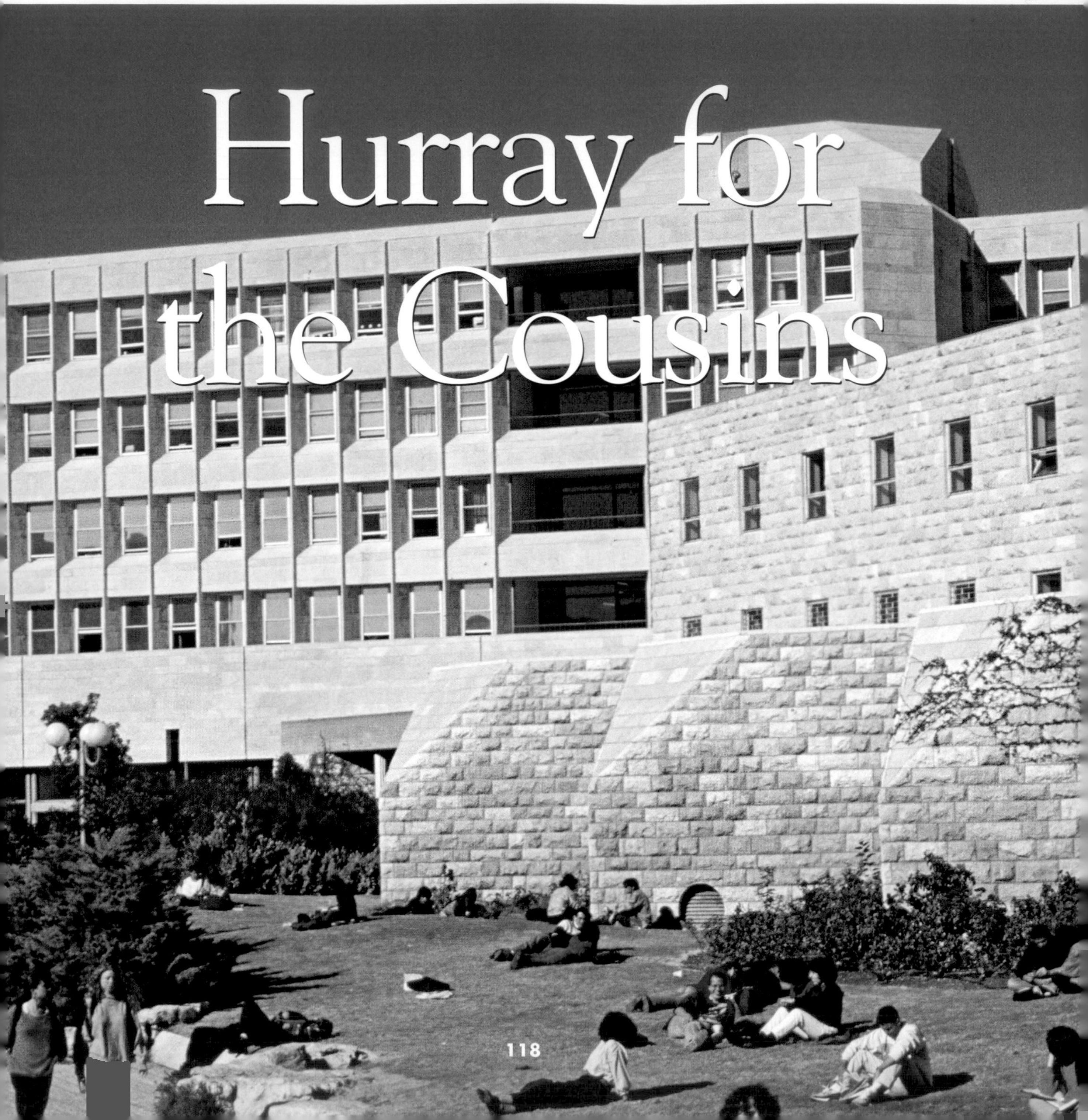

Aaron's family has just returned to Jerusalem from a year in Saint Paul, Minnesota, where his father, Ben, taught Middle Eastern art history at the University of Minnesota. Ben is now lecturing at the Hebrew University in Jerusalem, a short drive from their home. Aaron's mother, Ruth, is a sculptor. Several of her works are on display at the Jerusalem Artists' House on Shmuel Hanagid Street and at the Safrai Gallery on King David Street.

Opposite: **Students relax at the Hebrew University of Jerusalem. About twenty-four thousand students are enrolled at the university.**

Aaron is waiting for his cousins to arrive for a visit. While he waits, Aaron looks at a picture on the wall. It shows Uncle Chaim and his father with their arms around each other's shoulders. They are brothers, proudly wearing their army uniforms. Next to that picture is a photo of Grandpa and Grandma Hoffmann. In 1956, they came from South Africa to Haifa, where they still live. There is also a photo of Grandpa and Grandma Elazar, his mom's father and mother. They were born when Israel was still called Palestine, and they lived on a kibbutz near the Jordan River after they were married. Aaron never met them. They

Many Israeli artists show their work in tiny galleries on ancient streets.

died many years ago when a rocket hit their home during one of the wars Israel had with its Arab neighbors. Aaron's mother and her three sisters were working in Tel Aviv at the time and escaped injury. Aaron knows his mother and aunts still miss their parents, especially during holidays.

The Neighborhood

Aaron and his parents live in Ein Kerem, a neighborhood on the western heights of Jerusalem. Off to the left, above the nearby houses, Aaron can just see the top of a tower built above the Spring of the Virgin. His dad says that Mary, the mother of Jesus, supposedly drank water there. Although his family is Jewish, Aaron knows a lot about the Christian faith. Many of his friends back in the United States were Christian. He uses e-mail to keep in touch with them.

Home to Churches

Ein Kerem was once an Arab village, but it was abandoned to Jewish settlers after Israel gained its independence in 1948. Jerusalem eventually expanded to surround the tidy neighborhood. Ein Kerem is the home of several ancient Christian churches that are tourist attractions. Aaron is used to seeing buses stopping outside the Franciscan Church of St. John the Baptist, the Catholic Church of the Visitation, and the Russian Church. The sites are noted in guidebooks. Most of the visitors are older people. They always take a lot of pictures. One time, a woman from Canada took Aaron's photograph when he was walking past the Church of St. John the Baptist.

Several beautiful churches are located in Ein Kerem, including the Russian Church. It was built in 1888 by Alexander III, the leader of Russia, in memory of his mother.

Aaron was on his way to a soccer match when she asked if she could take his photo. Aaron was surprised when the woman's husband even gave him a shekel!

As the midmorning heat increases, the summer air becomes rich with a perfume from the rosebushes outside Aaron's front door. The blue sky overhead seems never-ending.

Dietary Laws

According to religious law, Orthodox Jews are not allowed to light fires on Saturday, the Sabbath. Hot food can be prepared the day before the Sabbath and then placed in a warm oven overnight. *Cholent*, a stew made with beans, potatoes, rice, and meat, is a popular Sabbath meal that is easy to prepare in that manner. Jews from North Africa add an extra twist by placing eggs on top of the stew. The eggs become hard-boiled as the stew cooks. A salad made with red and green peppers is served as a side dish, along with plenty of fresh fruit.

Kosher law also forbids Jews from eating pork and shellfish. Jews who keep kosher do not eat dairy products and meat at the same meal. They keep separate eating utensils for meat and dairy dishes.

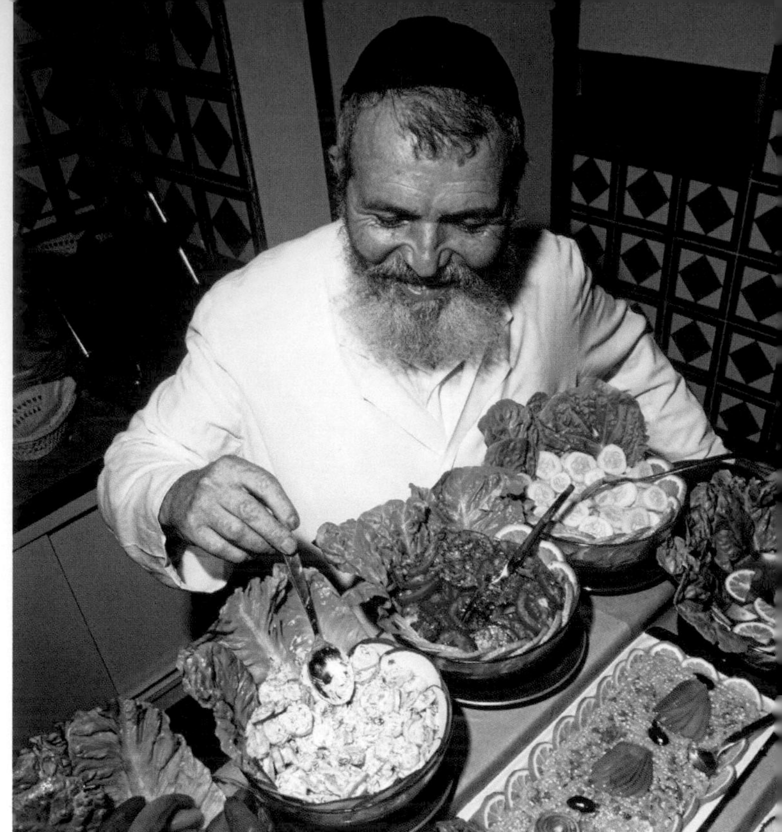

Friends

Outside, Aaron waves to Noah and Sammy, two of his school buddies who live down the road. They meet and talk with Asim, whose father is one of Israel's up-and-coming young Arab artists. They are ready to play soccer. Aaron and Asim favor Hapoel Jerusalem, the local professional team. Sammy likes Betar Jerusalem, and Noah roots for Hapoel Tel Aviv because he was born in the team's home city. Aaron's bedroom is papered with posters and photos of his favorite players.

A lot of painters, actors, and television personalities also live in Ein Kerem, a mixed area of Jewish, Muslim, and Christian professionals. Aaron's mom and dad know many of them through their work in the arts community.

From Jerusalem to a Kibbutz

Uncle Chaim, Aunt Lisa, and their children live on a kibbutz in the Judean Hills, where Chaim runs a tour service in the desert high above the Dead Sea. Aunt Lisa is a nurse on the kibbutz, a communal farm not far from the mountain fortress of Masada. Almost two thousand years ago, Jewish fighters killed themselves there rather than surrender to a Roman army. It is one of the most famous historical sites in Israel. Two years ago, Aaron spent a week with his cousins on the kibbutz. Uncle Chaim took everyone to Masada, and they rode a cable car up the mountainside.

Jerusalem doesn't have a cable car, but there is plenty to do there. The first thing Aaron plans to do is take his cousins

In ancient times, the best way to reach the top of Masada was to climb the "snake path" that zigzags up one side. Today, cable cars whisk visitors to the summit.

Israel's Official Holidays

The Jewish calendar has fewer days each year than the Gregorian calendar used in the United States and Canada, so the specific Western dates of Israel's holidays vary each year.

New Year of Trees	January–February
Purim	March
Passover	April
Holocaust Memorial Day	April–May
Memorial Day	April–May
Independence Day	April–May
Lag Ba'Omer	April–May
Jerusalem Day	May–June
Shavuot	May–June
Tisha B'Av	July–August
Rosh Hashana	September–October
Yom Kippur	September–October
Sukkot	September–October
Simchat Torah	October
Hanukkah	December

National Day is celebrated in November by the Palestinian Authority throughout the West Bank and the Gaza Strip. Ramadan is the most important Muslim holy season, when Muslims fast for an entire month. The Muslim calendar year is shorter than the Gergorian calendar year, so the dates of Ramadan fall at different times each year.

to the soccer field near Hadassah Hospital, where there is a funny-looking sculpture designed by Niki de Saint Phalle. The statue is a silly monster with three tongues. Each of the tongues is used as a slide by the little kids who live nearby. Aaron's dad once took him inside Hadassah Hospital to show him the stained-glass windows there. They were designed by the famous artist Marc Chagall. If they have time between kicking the soccer ball, Aaron will probably show his cousins the windows. He is sure they will be impressed.

According to the plan, Uncle Chaim and Aunt Lisa will drop off their children and drive home. Then, after the cousins' weeklong holiday in Jerusalem, Aaron's parents will take everyone back to the Ein Gedi kibbutz on the western rim of the Dead Sea, where the cousins live. The kibbutz is close to the Ein Gedi Nature Reserve, where Uncle Chaim often takes his tourist guests. Ein Gedi also has a beach and a resort. Both families plan on playing at Ein Gedi for a day. Aaron and his cousins have their hearts set on splashing in the huge outdoor swimming pool, and their parents are eager to have massages and take the mud treatments.

The Jerusalem Mall is a busy shopping center and well-known tourist attraction.

Urban Life

Aaron is used to a city's hustle and bustle. He doesn't mind the rushing traffic and loves the international flavor. Even though he is only in sixth grade, Aaron speaks English, Hebrew, and French and wants to study another language. Right now, he is thinking that he might want a job with the Israeli foreign service after he finishes college so he can travel some more. But that is a long way in the future.

Aaron enjoyed the week he spent in the desert with his cousins. He saw a gazelle, rode a camel, and bounced across the desert trails on his uncle's all-terrain vehicle. Now it is his turn to show off his city. Aaron and his parents have already worked out an itinerary. They are going to the Israel Museum, of course, where the kids' section has plenty of hands-on activities. The flashy, modern Jerusalem Mall, the largest shopping center in the Middle East, is also on the list. It is

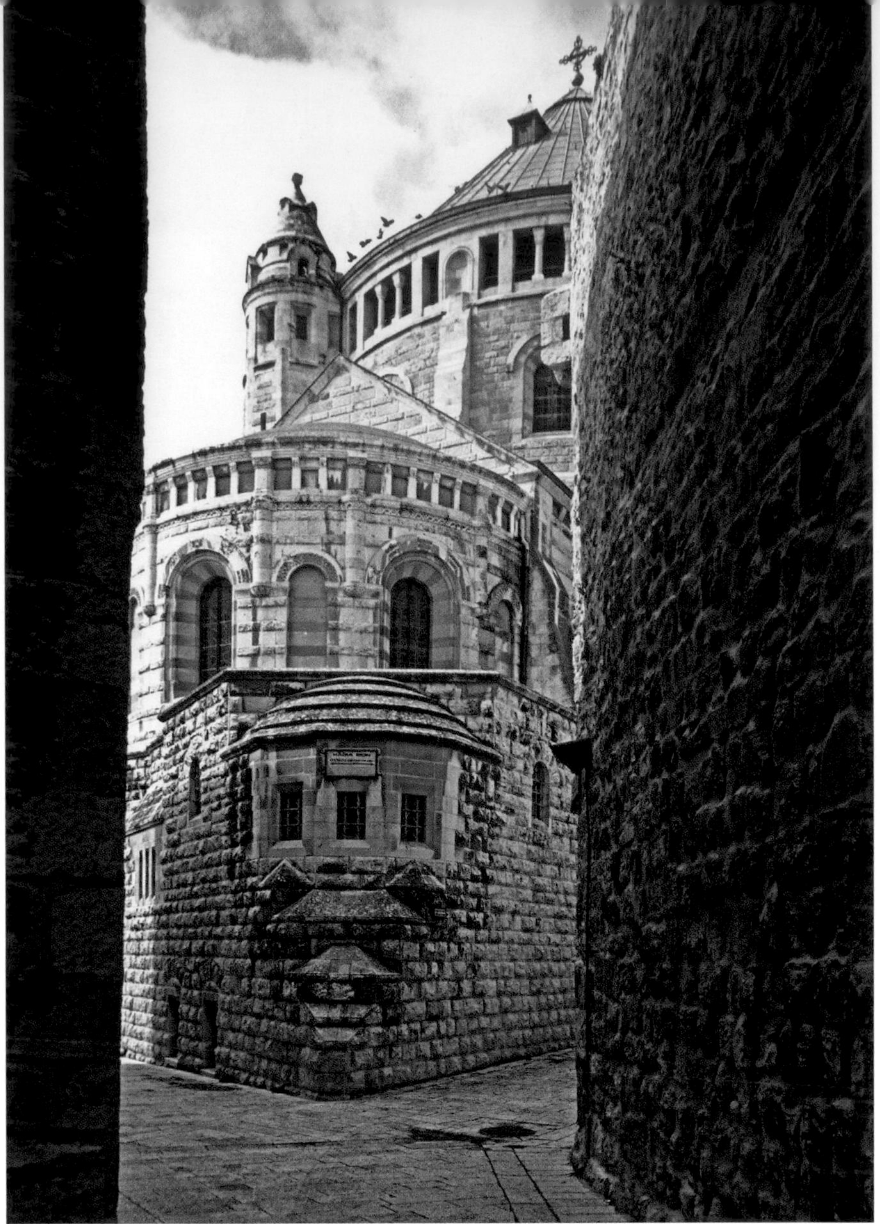

Jerusalem's Old City is filled with narrow streets and ancient buildings.

near the Teddy Kollek soccer stadium, one of Aaron's favorite places. The stadium is named after a popular longtime mayor of Jerusalem.

To balance the new with the old, Aaron and his cousins are going to walk through the narrow alleys of the Old City.

Their parents enjoy poking around the small shops and stalls, driving hard bargains when they see something they want. They are used to seeing armed soldiers on the street corners and rooftops, always on the alert for trouble.

Tastes and Smells

As Aaron awaits his cousins' arrival, a wonderful new aroma tickles his nose. His mom is preparing a great stack of snacks, knowing that everyone will be really hungry after their long car ride. She is baking *zalabi*, a buttered fritter sprinkled with brown sugar. Already on the kitchen table is a delicious honey cake, made with a mix of instant coffee, raisins, cloves, lemon peel, and all sorts of other ingredients. A bowl overflowing with ripe apples, bananas, oranges, dates, and kiwifruit rests on one side of the table. The only things missing are pomegranates, juicy red fruit with tiny seeds that snap when eaten. Aunt Lisa always brings extra pomegranates from their kibbutz. Aaron thinks they are the best in the world.

At last, Aaron hears the rumble of an engine from down the street. A large black truck with passenger seats boldly rounds the corner at the top of the hill, driven by a fellow with a great red beard. It's Uncle Chaim! "Hoffmann's Desert Tours" is splashed across both sides of his vehicle. The bright green lettering swirls around a picture of a galloping ibex. Assorted cousins hang out of every window. Chaim honks the horn and waves when he sees Aaron.

"They're here! They're here!" Aaron yells down to his folks. He hits the stairs running. It's time to see Jerusalem!

Timeline

Israeli History

Amorite clans populate Canaan (Israel).	3000 B.C.–2000 B.C.
Israelites conquer much of today's Israel.	1030 B.C.–931 B.C.
Alexander the Great conquers Israel.	332 B.C.
The Romans capture Jerusalem.	63 B.C.
Jesus is crucified outside Jerusalem.	ca. A.D. 33
Jerusalem is destroyed by the Romans; the Jews begin to disperse to other lands.	70
Jewish rebels commit suicide at Masada.	73
Muslim Arabs capture Palestine.	638
Christian Crusaders capture Jerusalem.	1099
Muslim leader Salah ad-din recaptures Jerusalem from the Crusaders.	1187
Ottoman Turks take control of Palestine.	1517

World History

2500 B.C.	Egyptians build the Pyramids and the Sphinx in Giza.
563 B.C.	The Buddha is born in India.
A.D. 313	The Roman emperor Constantine recognizes Christianity.
610	The Prophet Muhammad begins preaching a new religion called Islam.
1054	The Eastern (Orthodox) and Western (Roman) Churches break apart.
1066	William the Conqueror defeats the English in the Battle of Hastings.
1095	Pope Urban II proclaims the First Crusade.
1215	King John seals the Magna Carta.
1300s	The Renaissance begins in Italy.
1347	The Black Death sweeps through Europe.
1453	Ottoman Turks capture Constantinople, conquering the Byzantine Empire.
1492	Columbus arrives in North America.
1500s	The Reformation leads to the birth of Protestantism.
1776	The Declaration of Independence is signed.
1789	The French Revolution begins.

Israeli History

Eliezer Ben-Yehuda brings Hebrew to Palestine as a national language.	1881
The first kibbutz is founded at Degania.	1909
During World War I, the Turks are defeated; Britain occupies Palestine.	1914–1918
Britain issues the Balfour Declaration, stating that Jews have a right to a national home in Palestine.	1917
Hundreds of thousands of Jews immigrate to Palestine as anti-Semitism increases in Europe.	1930s
Britain restricts Jewish immigration into Palestine.	1939
More than 6 million European Jews are murdered during the Holocaust.	1939–1945
Israel becomes an independent nation.	1948
Israel attacks Egypt.	1956
Israel defeats Egypt, Syria, and Jordan in the Six-Day War.	1967
Egypt and Israel again go to war.	1973
Peace talks lead to Camp David Accords.	1978
Egypt and Israel sign a peace treaty.	1979
The Palestinian intifada begins.	1987
Prime Minister Yitzhak Rabin is assassinated.	1995
Israel pulls soldiers and settlers out of Gaza.	2005

World History

1865	The American Civil War ends.
1914	World War I breaks out.
1917	The Bolshevik Revolution brings communism to Russia.
1929	Worldwide economic depression begins.
1939	World War II begins, following the German invasion of Poland.
1945	World War II ends.
1957	The Vietnam War starts.
1969	Humans land on the moon.
1975	The Vietnam War ends.
1979	Soviet Union invades Afghanistan.
1983	Drought and famine in Africa.
1989	The Berlin Wall is torn down, as communism crumbles in Eastern Europe.
1991	Soviet Union breaks into separate states.
1992	Bill Clinton is elected U.S. president.
2000	George W. Bush is elected U.S. president.
2001	Terrorists attack World Trade Towers, New York, and the Pentagon, Washington, D.C.
2003	The U.S. invades Iraq.

Fast Facts

Official name: State of Israel
Capital: Jerusalem
Official languages: Hebrew and Arabic

Tel Aviv

Israel's flag

Wildflowers

National anthem:	"Hatikvah" ("The Hope")
Founding date:	May 14, 1948
Founder:	David Ben-Gurion, the first prime minister
Government:	Republic
Chief of state:	President
Head of government:	Prime minister
Area:	7,849 square miles (20,329 sq km)
Bordering countries:	Lebanon, Syria, Jordan, and Egypt
Highest elevation:	Mount Meron, 3,963 feet (1,208 m)
Lowest elevation:	Dead Sea, 1,312 feet (400 m) below sea level
Average temperatures:	January: 73°F (23°C) August: 80°F (27°C)
Average annual rainfall:	28 inches (71 cm) in the north and 2 inches (5 cm) in the south
National population (2005):	6,276,883

Population of largest cities (2004):

Jerusalem (including East Jerusalem)	680,500
Tel Aviv-Jaffa	360,500
Haifa	270,800
Rishon le-Ziyyon	211,600
Beersheba	181,500
Petah Tikva	176,600
Holon	165,800

The Dome of the Rock

Currency

Famous landmarks:

- ***Dome of the Rock***, Jerusalem
- ***Church of the Holy Sepulchre***, Jerusalem
- ***Western Wall***, Jerusalem
- ***Israel Museum***, Jerusalem
- ***Golda Meir Center for the Performing Arts***, Tel Aviv
- ***Dead Sea***

Industry: Israel's major industries include food processing; diamond cutting and polishing; and manufacturing of textiles, chemicals, metal products, and military equipment. The mining of potash is also important, as is tourism.

Currency: Israel's official currency is the Israeli new shekel. In 2005, one U.S. dollar equals 4.5 new shekels.

Weights and measures: Metric system

Literacy rate: About 100 percent

Common Hebrew words and phrases:

Shalom	Hello *or* Good-bye
Boker tov	Good morning
Erev tov	Good evening
Ken	Yes
Lo	No
Toda	Thank you
Bevakasha	Please *or* You're welcome

An Arab family

Golda Meir

Common Arabic words and phrases:	*Salaam aleikum*	Hello (formal)
	Marhaba	Hello (informal)
	Aleikum as-salaam	(response to "Hello")
	Sabah al-kheir	Good morning
	Masa' al-kheir	Good evening
	Aiwa	Yes
	La	No
	Shukran	Thank you
	Min fadlak	Please (to a man)
	Min fadlik	Please (to a woman)

Famous Israelis:	Shmuel Yosef Agnon *Author*	(1888–1970)
	Menachem Begin *Prime minister and Nobel Prize winner*	(1913–1992)
	David Ben-Gurion *Prime minister*	(1886–1973)
	Hayim Nahman Bialik *Poet*	(1873–1934)
	Gal Fridman *Olympic champion windsurfer*	(1975–)
	Golda Meir *Prime minister*	(1898–1978)
	Itzhak Perlman *Musician*	(1945–)
	Ariel Sharon *Prime minister*	(1928–)
	Ido Tadmor *Dancer*	(1964–)

To Find Out More

Nonfiction

- Burstein, Chaya M. *A Kid's Catalog of Israel*. Philadelphia: Jewish Publication Society, 1998.
- Corona, Laurel. *Israel*. San Diego: Lucent Books, 2003.
- DuBois, Jill. *Israel*. New York: Benchmark Books, 2004.
- Ellis, Deborach. *Three Wishes: Palestinian and Israeli Children Speak*. Toronto: Groundwood Books, 2004.
- Finkelstein, Norman H. *Ariel Sharon*. Minneapolis: Lerner Publications Company, 2005.
- Pasachoff, Naomi. *Links in the Chain: Shapers of the Jewish Tradition*. New York: Oxford University Press, 1998.
- Rivlin, Lilly, with Gila Gevritz. *Welcome to Israel*. Springfield, N.J.: Behrman House, 2000.
- Waldman, Neil. *Masada*. New York: HarperCollins Publishers, 1998.

Fiction

- Benderly, Beryl Lieff. *Jason's Miracle: A Hanukkah Story*. Morton Grove, Ill.: Albert Whitman, 2000.
- Konigsburg, E. L. *About the B'Nai Bagels*. New York: Yearling Publishing/Random House, 1985.
- Konigsburg, E. L. *Up from Jericho Tel*. New York: Aladdin, 1998.

Web Sites

- **Aleph-Bet**
  http://www.morim.com/games.htm
  For language games to learn Hebrew

- **Israel Ministry of Foreign Affairs**
  http://www.mfa.gov.il/mfa
  For all sorts of information about the government and history of Israel

- **Israel Museum Youth Wing**
  http://www.imj.org.il/eng/youth
  For information about classes, exhibits, and activities at the museum

- **Torah.net/Jewish Youth Center**
  http://www.torah.net/eng/kids
  For short stories, jokes, and facts about Judaism

- **Zemerl**
  http://www.zemerl.com
  An interactive site with Jewish songs in English, Yiddish, and Ladino (Judeo-Spanish)

Organizations

- **Embassy of Israel**
  3514 International Drive NW
  Washington, DC 20008
  202/364-5527

- **Israel Ministry of Tourism Information Center**
  800 Second Avenue
  New York, NY 10017
  212/499-5660
  888/77ISRAEL

Index

Page numbers in *italics* indicate illustrations.

I

J

K

L

Meet the Author

Martin Hintz is a long-time writer and editor. He is the author of almost a hundred books on topics ranging from monster trucks to the story of Prohibition. He has also written numerous award-winning cultural geographies in the Enchantment of the World series.

Hintz contributes articles to dozens of magazines and newspapers in the United States and abroad, concentrating on travel, outdoor adventure, personalities, and arts. He also publishes *The Irish American Post* magazine, which deals with Irish and Irish American affairs, and manages the Mountjoy Writers Group, an international news and features syndicate. Hintz is a past president of the Society of American Travel Writers and is active in other organizations such as the Society of Professional Journalists, the Committee to Protect Journalists, and the Milwaukee Press Club.

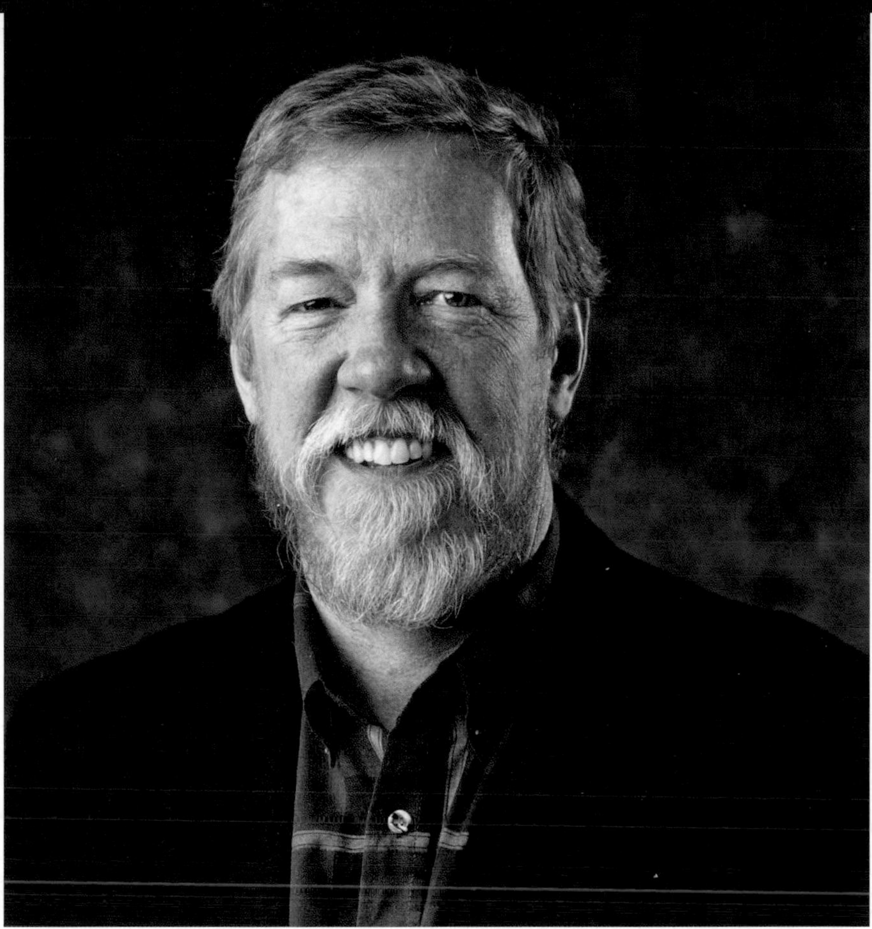

Hintz has visited Israel several times on writing assignments. He is also the author of *Images of America: Jewish Milwaukee*, which touches on the world of Jewish immigrants, their families' subsequent rise in society, and their ongoing relationship with Israel.

Hintz and his wife, Pam, live near Milwaukee, Wisconsin, where they raise chickens and share their house with a large Maine coon cat named Tom. The couple has climbed the heights of Masada, parasailed on the Red Sea, and explored Jerusalem's Old City, meeting and talking with Israelis of all professions.

Photo Credits

Photographs © 2006:

Alamy Images: 31 (Chris Gomersall), 32, 89 (Eitan Simanor), 28 (World Religions Photo Library)

AP/Wide World Photos: 99 (Oded Balilty), 60 top (Jerome Delay), 53 (Ron Edmonds), 14, 133 top (Enric Marti), 57 (Paul Miller), 43 (PID/Zionistisches Archiv), 54, 59, 133 bottom

Art Resource, NY: 39 (Erich Lessing), 40 (Snark)

Bruce Coleman Inc./Eitan Simanor: 62

Corbis Images: 13 (Khaled al-Hariri/Reuters), 122 (Dave Bartruff), 80 (Morton Beebe), 76 (Natalie Behring/Reuters), 103 (Annie Griffiths Belt), 41, 45, 55, 81 (Bettmann), 100 (Bojan Brecelj), 60 bottom, 118, 121 (Shai Ginott), 119 (Dave G. Houser), 35, 47 (Hulton-Deutsch Collection), 12, 20, 33, 115 (Hanan Isachar), 107 (Ed Kashi), 21, 29 (Steve Kaufman), 73 (Douglas Kirkland), 30 (Frans Lemmens/zefa), 69 top (James Marshall), 104 (Michael Nicholson), 17, 22 right (Richard T. Nowitz), 75, 132 bottom (Christine Osborne), 123 (Carl & Ann Purcell), 52 (Ricki Rosen), 77, 105 (Ricki Rosen/SABA), 91 (David Rubinger), 110 (Ron Sachs), 84 (Stephanie Sinclair), 7 bottom, 90 (Ted Spiegel), 51

Getty Images: 79 (Tal Cohen/AFP), 48 (Charles Hewitt/Hulton Archive), 37 (Hulton Archive), 101 (Abid Katib), 71 (David Rubinger/Time Life Pictures), 86, 117 (David Silverman), 116 (Ian Walton)

Images & Stories: 92 (Murat Germen), 22 left, 64, 126, 130 left (Izzet Keribar), 18 (Fatih Pinar)

ImageState: 102, 132 top (Jean-Erick Pasquier/Rapho), 9 (Philippe Roy/HOA-QUI), 93

Index Stock Imagery: 11, 26, 67, 85, 94, 131 bottom (ASAP Ltd.), 74 (Yvette Cardozo), 7 top, 16 (Barry Winiker)

Israelimages.com: 44 (Lev Borodulin), 111 (Diggy Dekel), 66 (Kenneth Fisher), 108 (GPO), 113 (Douglas Guthrie), 25, 78 (Naftali Hilger), 34, 112 (Hanan Isachar), 69 bottom (Itsik Marom), 96, 97, 98, 125 (Israel Talby)

Lonely Planet Images: 2 (Paul David Hellander), 82 (Oliver Strewe)

MapQuest.com, Inc.: 56, 131 top

National Geographic Image Collection: 8 (Kenneth Garrett), 27 (James L. Stanfield), 10 (Maynard Owen Williams)

Ron Gang, artist, Kibbutz Urim, Israel, www.rongang.net: 106, 114

Superstock, Inc.: cover, 6 (Yoshio Tomii), 23 (Steve Vidler)

The Image Works: 109 (ArenaPal/Topham), 36, 42 (Topham)

Maps by XNR Productions, Inc.